GATEWAY TO THE
OUTER BANKS

Dawson Carr

The University of North Carolina Press

CHAPEL HILL

This book was published with the assistance of the
Blythe Family Fund
of the University of North Carolina Press.

Designed by Kimberly Bryant
Set in Miller by Tseng Information Systems, Inc.
Manufactured in the United States of America

Cover illustrations: (top) old car crossing wooden bridge,
Outer Banks History Center, D. Victor Meekins Collection; (middle) the
town of Corolla before it was reached by NC 12, Outer Banks History
Center, Aycock Brown Collection; (bottom) aerial view of Bonner Bridge,
Outer Banks History Center, Drew Wilson Collection.

Library of Congress Cataloging-in-Publication Data
Carr, Dawson, author.
NC 12 : gateway to the Outer Banks / Dawson V. Carr.
pages cm
Includes bibliographical references and index.
ISBN 978-1-4696-2814-1 (pbk : alk. paper) —
ISBN 978-1-4696-2815-8 (ebook)
1. Outer Banks (N.C.)—History. 2. Roads—North Carolina—
Outer Banks. 3. Tourism—North Carolina—Outer Banks. I. Title.
F262.096C37 2016
975.6′1—dc23
2015031960

To my grandchildren,

BRANDI CARR, TREVOR CARR,

ANDREW SCHRODT, JORDAN SCHRODT,

and DEVIN CARR,

Who are my route to the future

CONTENTS

MAPS

PREFACE

The story of Highway 12 on North Carolina's Outer Banks is the story not just of a road, but of a place. The Banks and the road are linked so intricately that it is difficult to consider one without the other. They exist in harmony, and as one goes, so goes the other. Their fates are bonded almost symbiotically, and their futures are bound together.

It was not always so.

In the years before automobiles became common, the wide expanses of water that separated the Outer Banks from the mainland were a formidable barrier for most travelers, even the few who tried to get there by boat. No docks or ports awaited arriving ships anywhere on the Banks, and those that tried to get by Cape Hatteras were often waylaid by the notorious underwater dunes called Diamond Shoals. Most visits, then, were purely unintentional and often disastrous. Not until well into the twentieth century did people begin to travel to the Outer Banks in automobiles, which required two things: access to the islands and a road to drive on once there. This book tells the amazing story of how that access and that road were imagined, developed, and maintained.

Like automobiles, I came late to the Outer Banks. In 1967 a couple of friends invited me on a trip to Ocracoke, a place I had heard of but did not know much about. We left one afternoon, drove the couple hundred miles to the eastern edge of the state, and spent the night at Cedar Island. The next day, we rode the ferry across Pamlico Sound to reach Ocracoke village. We checked into the Island Inn, a quaint, attractive lodging with very good rates—perhaps because there was no heat in the rooms and it was the dead of winter.

We drove down shady, enchanting lanes to reach the nearby beach and quickly found the timbers of a long-lost sailing ship sticking out of the sands. The ancient vessel had been put together with wooden pegs, and I snitched one of the pegs as a souvenir. From there, we drove to a small graveyard where four British sailors were buried; the sign hanging on the surrounding fence noted that because of the bodies buried there, it would always be a part of England. It was a touching scene.

The town was small and comforting, and the Ocracoke Lighthouse stood just beyond the center of the village. The natural, scenic beauty of the place was remarkable. I was immediately sold on the idea of vacationing on the Outer Banks, although life's vagaries and my work schedule did not allow me to return for nearly twenty years. When I finally returned one November with my parents and my wife to visit other parts of the famed region, some areas had changed, though much was still the same. After we crossed the bridge from Roanoke Island, we arrived at NC Highway 12 at Whalebone Junction, an intriguing name for the little intersection just south of Nags Head. We traveled from there northward a few miles to Kitty Hawk, where we had reserved a cottage. The little house was of simple design but sat high on supporting posts that kept it well above any ocean water that might reach there should a storm arise. It was not on the beach but on a small connecting road between the two parallel highways, NC 12 and the bypass. Still, it was not far from the Atlantic Ocean and its threatening waves.

A few decades earlier, there had been a high sand ridge between the beach and the cottages, but that had gradually eroded away, and even many of the former houses that lined the inviting oceanfront had been washed out of existence as well. The extensive commercial development that would follow in years to come had not yet been completed, and it was a peaceful, uncrowded environment. Some of the older cottages that had been eliminated by time and weather were gradually being replaced by newer, more expensive abodes, but the oceanfront was not yet enveloped by them and the beach was visible from NC 12. Riding along the highway, which was uncongested in those days, was practically carefree and allowed one to see the businesses and historic sites with ease. And there was much to see even then, including an attractive off-the-road restaurant sitting beside the sound waters, where we enjoyed our Thanksgiving meal in relaxed comfort and almost-home-cooked style. Although the area has grown tremendously since those years, many restaurants there still have the same down-home atmosphere.

We visited the Wright Brothers Memorial, which was not far away and whose tall monument could be seen from the highway, and we also traveled back across the bridge to see and board the replica of Sir Walter Raleigh's ship, *Elizabeth II*. The small but well-maintained road labeled as NC 12 led us across the bridge over Oregon Inlet after passing the Bodie Island Lighthouse, which we did not explore since visitors were not invited inside in those days. The road continued all the way to Cape Hatteras, where the tallest brick lighthouse in America stood at the very edge of the sea. No one could have known or even imagined then that this lighthouse would one day be moved a half mile back to safety. Its spiraling stripes caught the eye long before it was close enough to climb.

The island was so narrow, it was amazing that a highway could have been constructed there at all, particularly in a place so far from the mainland. It seemed to me a miracle road, not only in its existence but because it opened the way to so many historic sites. It was while we were traveling along NC 12 on that trip that my idea to someday tell its story began to germinate. The idea developed gradually, spreading across more years than I want to believe. One thing was sure: with millions of tourists riding on NC 12 every year, this road spanning the Outer Banks is comparable to any renowned highway in any location, and its story is worthy of telling.

I learned a great deal in the investigation of what is known locally as the "Beach Road," but I also found much to worry about concerning its future and that of the Outer Banks themselves. That side of the story deserves consideration as well. This book examines how NC 12 came into being, what effects it has had, how it has endured, and what the future might hold, not only for the road but also for the region it traverses. The final chapter includes a narrative of what it is like to ride the notable road from one end to the other.

My two friends who first showed me the wonders of the Outer Banks are gone now, but I will always be grateful to them for opening the way for me to enjoy such an amazing place. They knew of NC 12 long before I did and introduced me to it, and I hope to return the favor in some small way through the pages of this book. I invite you to take a historic ride with me along the Outer Banks and its little ribbon of pavement known as NC 12, and perhaps also treat yourself to a tour of the actual road that still stands precariously atop the Atlantic sands.

■ Many people are involved in the writing of a book, and several have assisted me in the preparation of *NC 12*. It would have been unlikely if not impossible to prepare it without them, and I thank all who participated. The names of some have slipped from my memory, but their contributions are not forgotten.

Some who were especially helpful will be mentioned here to show their participation and to give me the opportunity to express my appreciation. First, many members of the staff at the University of North Carolina Press provided help whenever it was needed, which was often. Those include Zach Read, Lucas Church, Jay Mazzocchi, and others. But my main guiding force came from Mark Simpson-Vos, editorial director, who took me under his wing early and stuck with me throughout the struggles. When my writing started to ramble and get off course, he patiently guided me back to the proper direction. The UNC Press author's guide, *STET,* was a lifesaver for someone who took a single typing course many years ago and whose level of technical knowledge was overwhelmed with the advent of word processing and computers. Although their names were not divulged, the two readers who read the manuscript provided valuable help in revising and correcting areas where I inadvertently erred. It is always helpful to have the eyes of others look things over when your own vision is hampered by having looked at the material so much.

My son, Greg, provided me with the technical equipment I needed, including both a laptop and a desktop computer. Even with my lack of skill, I was able to do things with those contraptions that I never dreamed possible. I called him so frequently for help with the devices that he finally had to tell me they did not come with tech support. However, he faithfully assisted me whenever necessary. I also thank my daughter, Becky Schrodt, and her son Andrew for helping me with word-processing problems I encountered and with getting the printers to obey my commands. Both of them came whenever I called and showed me the ways of technology that always seemed just beyond my grasp. When a serious computer virus snuck into my computer in the dark of night and encrypted my entire manuscript, Joanna Garcia of Microsoft stayed on the phone off and on with me over a span of two days to help get it all sorted out.

Several folks on the Outer Banks allowed me to interview them while I was researching the history of NC 12 and the Banks themselves. My wife and I were honored to be invited into the home of the late David Stick, who told us stories of the history of the area. I regard him as the foremost authority on Outer Banks history and have read most of his books; it was a pleasant encounter, as well as informative, hearing him relate some of that history in person. Tim Midgett of Hatteras Island invited us in for an interview in his real estate office, where he shared stories of early automobile use on Hatteras Island. He allowed me to borrow and read his family scrapbook that covered the years the Midgett bus line operated on the island before and after the advent of a paved road there. Some of his accounts are included in this book. Coleman and Ann Ragsdale of Nags Head welcomed us into their beach cottage and told us tales of the olden days on the Banks. Throughout, I was glad to have the excuse of writing this book, since it gave me a reason for hearing all those fascinating narratives and for meeting all those interesting people.

Many members of the North Carolina Department of Transportation (NCDOT) talked to me and gave me requested information regarding the history of NC 12. Workers at the Ferry Division always took the time to answer my numerous questions and did so with patience and courtesy. I especially thank Sterling Baker and Kayren N. Williamson, who sent me pictures or maps when they were needed. I am thankful to all the members of NCDOT, for without their dedicated efforts to maintain the Beach Road, NC 12, there would be no story to tell.

One of my favorite spots on the Outer Banks is the Outer Banks History Center in Manteo, and I spent many pleasant hours there researching the history of the road. The personnel there were always dependable, knowledgeable, and friendly. Much of the information in this book came from the files there, as did many of the illustrations. I want to thank KaeLi Schurr, who helped me then and also later when I had to call back for clarifications, as well as Tama Creef and Sarah Downing (who has now moved to another location). They guided my efforts and made my research more efficient. A special note of thanks goes to Stuart Parks II, who not only prepared the digital forms of the photos and provided them for me with care and organization but also gave me my first information about Project Nutmeg, of which I knew nothing. The Outer Banks Chamber of Commerce has given me information about populations of the various villages on the Outer Banks and has helped supply other relevant information upon request. I credit them for their assistance and for the value of their information.

Two of my friends who are successful professional writers, Stephen Smith and Sara King, volunteered to read some of the manuscript and offer guidance when I was struggling. And I will always be thankful to my two late friends, former senator Harris Blake and fellow educator Gerald Thomas, who first introduced me to the wonders of the Outer Banks and to NC 12.

Newspapers have been listed frequently as sources in the manuscript, but I would like to say that I especially found much information in the *Coastland Times*, the *Virginian-Pilot*, and the *Raleigh News and Observer*. All are dedicated followers of activities affecting the Outer Banks and their highway.

Finally, I thank my wife, Bobbi, who helped me with numerous tasks when I was unable to manage some process or procedure alone, and who has been extremely patient with me during the time I spent trying to write this book. She understood during the occasional times, which I claim were quite rare, when my attention wandered. She also forgave me for the many household chores I had to neglect. I am not sure what excuse I can use now.

The people who have assisted in this venture, the chronicles I have heard, and the things I have witnessed have made the Outer Banks even more enchanting to me. If the story has been told in a way befitting all the accounts and guidance given to me by so many thoughtful people, and if the details of North Carolina's Outer Banks and NC 12 are portrayed as they deserve to be, you might find this book as interesting to read as it was to write.

PROLOGUE

We were cut off from everything—from the rest of the state,
and the rest of the country; why the different parts of
Dare County were cut off from each other. The only way to get to
Hatteras or Kitty Hawk, or the mainland, was by boat.
—Wash Baum from David Stick,
The Outer Banks of North Carolina

North Carolina's legendary Outer Banks are in some danger. This is nothing new given their isolated and precarious location, but increasingly rapid rises in sea levels in recent years have put all of the exposed coastal areas of the world under an escalating threat of destruction or even elimination, and it is hard to imagine a more exposed region than the Outer Banks. Made up of a thin band of sand barely higher than the sea itself, the outlying ridge squirms and reshapes itself with every passing storm, waiting uncertainly for the storms that will follow.

A hundred years ago, most people knew little about the Outer Banks and probably cared less what might happen to them. That does not include the islands' few permanent residents, who undoubtedly would have been very concerned but whose voices likely would have gone unheard. All of this changed with the building of bridges from the mainland and the paving of a road from the far northern tip to the lower extremes of the Banks.

Until those developments took place, some regarded the region as a kind of wasteland that had little value as real estate and too small of a population to merit special attention. So, in 1949, it was only natural for the U.S. military to look upon the Outer Banks as virtually empty and ideal for a special mission they had in mind. It had become too expensive and troublesome to use the distant Marshall Islands for testing the latest nuclear devices, and a more desirable location on the U.S. continent was needed. The program to seek out and find such a locale was called "Project Nutmeg." Those in charge of the project eyed the remote, desolate region off the North Carolina coast with excitement: the Outer Banks looked like the perfect testing site for atomic weapons.

North Carolina and the U.S. military have always had a strong and ongoing relationship, with major bases like Fort Bragg, Camp Lejeune, and Seymour Johnson well-known within and outside the state. It was natural to consider North Carolina once more for a new planned site. But because the Banks had been so isolated and relatively unknown, military leaders knew little of the true situation there or of the history of the area.

The Outer Banks had been among the first places the English selected in their attempt to establish colonies in the New World. The great reach of the Banks out into the Atlantic along the shipping routes of early explorers naturally caught their eye as a quick and easy place to put a settlement. In fact, Sir Walter Raleigh did send a group from England in 1587 to establish the first colony on Roanoke Island, just inside an inlet that led through the Banks near where Nags Head is today. Unfortunately, the colony mysteriously disappeared within three years and was doomed to be known thereafter as "The Lost Colony." While it was there, though, Roanoke Island became the birthplace of Virginia Dare, the first English child known to be born in America. She vanished along with the rest of the colonists, but several features and places on the Outer Banks still bear her name.

Long before any explorers arrived from Europe, Native Americans made their home on the Outer Banks. Recent archaeological evidence indicates they had been there for more than a thousand years. Members of the Woccon, Croatoan, and Hatterask Tribes lived on the island chain, where the abundance of seafood made life rich and the remoteness from the mainland gave some protection from warfare.

The Outer Banks, then, had long been populated despite their distance from the mainland and the difficulties in traveling to and from them. After the Tuscarora War ended around 1715, Native Americans left the Outer Banks. Most appear to have joined other tribes in what are now the northern states, but a few still remain in isolated communities within North Carolina. This migration left the region open to settlement by Europeans, though few chose to live there.

Because of the abundance of fish in the sound and ocean waters, a few fishermen and their families began to settle on the Banks, and whales came near enough to the shores to inspire some whaling in the region. The large number of ships that sailed close by, as well as the numerous inlets and sounds that offered hiding places, enticed pirates to establish bases in the region from which they could lie in wait in their fast ships and rush out to attack and loot passing vessels. Because Ocracoke Inlet, and later Oregon Inlet, gave access to North Carolina port towns, pilots were needed to guide ships through the treacherous passages leading to and from places like Bath and Edenton. The southern tip of Ocracoke Island was an easy place to board the ships, so pilots took up residence there, producing a small permanent population.

There seemed to be little interest among outsiders to try to get to the Outer Banks or move to the area. The vast surrounding waters of the sounds prevented easy travel, and traveling by foot or oxcart from Virginia was inconvenient. The inaccessibility of the Banks kept the population of Europeans and their descendants low for centuries.

The military planners hatching Project Nutmeg in 1949 believed such was still the case. What they did not know was that after the Wright brothers came to Kitty Hawk and Kill Devil Hills in the early twentieth century for their experiments in flight, their success had brought sudden and widespread fame not only to them but also to the place they had chosen to work. Eventually, this led to the building of bridges and roads that brought in thousands of visitors and hundreds of new residents. Almost overnight, the remote, barely populated Outer Banks were converted into a thriving economy with significant business and housing development.

Project Nutmeg officials wrongly determined that there were only a few inhabitants on the Outer Banks, and they could be moved to new locations so that the barrier-island chain would be clear for the large number of tests planned for the next few years. They stated that the tests—detonating nuclear weapons on towers or airdropping them onto designated target zones on the Banks—would do little damage to the wildlife or fisheries there, and that people as a whole were irrationally concerned about the long-term effects of radioactivity from nuclear blasts. The project leaders also failed to consider the extensive schools of fish that roamed the area and laid their eggs in the adjacent sounds and the huge flights of geese and other birds that used the area for wintering and survival. The question of sea turtles probably never even came up.

So there appeared to be no problems with choosing the Outer Banks for the nuclear testing program, and no one would be able to protest the choice until it was too late since Project Nutmeg was top secret. Some of the officers making the decision were quite enthusiastic about how well the narrow coastal landform met the necessary conditions for the proposed testing and offered their support to proceed. Before the decision could be finalized, however, Gordon Dean, the newly named director of the Atomic Energy Commission, had aerial photographs taken of the entire Outer Banks region around 1950 so he could study the area himself. Upon close examination of the images, he noticed that a road had been built there and, as a result, development was considerable. It was not such a desolate, unpopulated area after all. These contemporary views of the barrier islands depicted a region that was quite different from what had been assumed, and Dean was adamant that the area was unsuitable as a base for Project Nutmeg. Ultimately, the military chose a desert area of Nevada as the site of their nuclear testing project. The Outer Banks had narrowly escaped.

Today, the Outer Banks are not out of danger, nor is the road that the director saw in the photographs; but those who, with all good intent, seek to protect the Banks from natural or human-related destruction might want to consider the past and be thankful that things are as good as they are. While a fate involving overconstruction of buildings or submersion by rising waves due to climate change is definitely of grave concern, exposure to continual devastating blasts of nuclear bombs that would have left only a string of craters where sand and land used to be, and residual radiation that would bar any visitation by people or wildlife for years to come, was arguably much worse. The admonitions by a few that the Outer Banks Highway, NC 12, is a threat to the barrier islands must be countered to some extent by the realization that at one critical point in history, it was that very road that saved them.

The Outer Banks remain as welcoming as ever, though they are growing more fragile with passing years and rising seas. The road that spared them nuclear destruction and helped spread the message of their beauty and importance still endures as well. Let us now travel back to see exactly how the region and the road developed and grew together.

CHAPTER

1

SHIFTING SANDS
AND CHALLENGING MODES
OF TRANSPORTATION

North Carolina's Outer Banks are a storied land where ruth-less pirates once roamed and wild Spanish mustangs wan-dered freely. The pirates are gone now, and the mustangs are not as free as they once were, but the Banks themselves still stretch far from the mainland out into the Atlantic Ocean, where they are pitted against that mighty sea in an eternal struggle for survival.

The narrow tendril of land hangs suspended southward from the Virginia shores and separates the ocean from the vast sound waters to the west, serving as a fence that shields not only the waters of the sounds but also the mainland shores of North Carolina from the threat of the waves. But those waves, as well as steady ocean currents, nibble relent-lessly at the narrow landform that is the Outer Banks, threat-ening to obliterate the skinny ridge of sand with each passing storm. Photographs from space portray an image of frailty that seems to confirm the dangers, but that is an illusion, for the Outer Banks have survived the assaults of and coexisted with the stormy Atlantic for several thousand years. Yet, the struggle is not without effects, for sand is continually eroded by the waves, and inlets are washed through the little strip of sand from time to time. As the sand is washed or blown over the Banks and pours through the inlets, it accumu-lates on the westward side, so that as the eastern side erodes and shrinks, the western side harvests the transported sand and grows. This has led to a gradual movement of the Outer Banks toward the west over the millennia, and it is a process that continues today.

The Banks themselves, which stand as a barricade to the Atlantic, are composed of tiny bits of stone chiseled by time and weather from the faraway Blue Ridge Mountains. Carried to the location by rivers through the ages, these granules of quartz and feldspar are mixed there with the shattered remnants of shells of countless departed sea creatures whose only proof of existence lies in the blended residue called sand. The willowy landform bulges out conspicuously from mainland North Carolina in an arc that encloses over 3,000 square miles of fresh and brackish waters of estuaries, marshes, and sounds, forming perhaps the most prominent coastline of the eastern seaboard of the United States.

By proper definition, the Outer Banks are a barrier-island chain, but the exact origin of their structure is still a matter of conjecture even among scientists. Many believe the formation emerged from the sea after the ending of the last Ice Age, either caused by or coincident with that event. Most scientists agree that the melting of glaciers around the world poured huge quantities of water into the oceans, raising sea levels and eating at shorelines everywhere. As a result, the Atlantic Ocean has marched westward over the past few thousand years and in the process has inundated the eastern coastline of what is now the United States, submerging shorelines, carving out giant concave bights with pointed capes, and reshaping river mouths and deltas. One holdout against the rising water, where the land still seemed to be trying to hold its own despite encroachment from the sea, was the outer edge of North Carolina.

Rising water from melting glaciers has raised sea levels as much as 400 feet in recent millennia, and some surmise that the higher ocean, combined with long-shore currents skirting the Carolina coast, rolled the deep sand from the continental shelf into the narrow, elongated mound that became the

Outer Banks. No matter what their origin, the Outer Banks are still there today, writhing in slow motion through the centuries and moving slowly but steadily toward the west as sea levels continue to rise. North Carolina's Outer Banks have become the most salient feature of that state and perhaps of the entire U.S. eastern coastline. The archipelago encloses the northern half of the North Carolina coast from the Virginia border to Ocracoke Island and beyond. The slender ridge of sand is rarely more than three miles wide and in places shrinks to just a few hundred yards. At such narrow places, one can stand in the middle of the strip and see water on both sides. Despite its slight dimensions, the serpentine ribbon of sand manages to protect the mainland from the violent waves of the Atlantic while corralling the flows of more than half a dozen rivers, including the Chowan, Pamlico, Neuse, and Alligator. In the process, it causes the submergence of huge portions of the low-lying region to create immense drowned lands known as the Albemarle, Currituck, Pamlico, Croatan, and Roanoke Sounds. Some early explorers who saw the extensive waters of the sounds believed them to be another ocean, but they are shallow from the accumulation of sand dumped there by the Banks's confinement of the rivers and are more like a giant lake than an ocean.

The Outer Banks exist in a region where the mixing of sand and water is constant. The gradual movement toward the west and the opening and refilling of inlets is an ongoing process, for despite their resilience, the Outer Banks are not immune to attack; storms have ripped them asunder numerous times, gouging inlets between ocean and sound. Storms swoop in from the sea at times to strike the Banks with monstrous waves and powerful winds that drive immense quantities of water across the lithe landform in its thinnest places. The overwash can increase the volume of water in the sounds to unsustainable levels, so that once the storm moves on and the wind changes direction, excess liquid gushes back across the strand to slice channels through the sand, opening outlets—ironically known as inlets—to the sea. After inlets form,

Early visitors to the Outer Banks faced deep, abiding sand in almost every direction, which impeded travel by automobiles. (Courtesy of the Outer Banks History Center, David Stick Collection)

sand continues to flow in and out of the channels, but some sand accumulates as it falls along the way, until after a time, the inlets are refilled and the strip is welded back together again. Thus regions like Bodie Island and Pea Island are still called islands long after the inlets that defined them have disappeared.

Because of the remoteness of the Outer Banks and their isolation from the mainland, the population of residents of European descent remained low for about 200 years. Movement to and from there was almost entirely by boat during those times, although it was possible to travel along the northern spit from Virginia by foot, on horseback, or in riding carts pulled by oxen. Those who did choose to live on the

Banks struggled to survive. Some farmed, others fished, and all reaped the benefits of shipwrecks that were so common in the region, which was to become known as the Graveyard of the Atlantic. Salvaging from wrecked vessels was not illegal, and locals often rescued crew members and passengers of lost ships. Banks residents sometimes clothed and fed those unfortunates from their own meager supplies, thus providing salvation for castaways who had little other hope for survival on the distant shores.

It was, in fact, shipwrecks that eventually led to an increase in the population of the Outer Banks and to a growth in their economy as well. During the nineteenth century, the U.S. government began the construction of four lighthouses on the Banks to guide ships along the edge of the barrier islands and especially around notorious Diamond Shoals, where hundreds of proud ships met their doom. It was a much-needed move to alleviate the extraordinary losses of ships, cargoes, passengers, and crew along North Carolina's shores, where Cape Hatteras was known as one of the most dangerous shipping areas in the world. Locals were often employed to manage lighthouse operations, and outsiders who were hired brought their families to live there, leading to a small increase in population and added income for the area.

Additional government actions began in 1871, when the U.S. Congress established the Lifesaving Service. As a result of that legislation, by 1874 seven lifesaving stations were located on the Outer Banks. Mostly locals who were familiar with the area were hired to operate the lifesaving activities, but a few outsiders were attracted there, too.

The gradual growth of population also led to an increase of construction on the Banks. Most residents built their homes on the western side of the barrier-island chain, where they could gain some sanctuary from the frequent storms. It was there that a few hotels to accommodate visitors were established as well. That made it convenient for travelers, who primarily came by boat and landed at docks near the hotels. Towns subsequently grew on the western side, and rails were

Often, after severe storms, the skeletons of old ships wash out of the sands, providing ample evidence of the danger the Outer Banks posed to sailors and their vessels as they attempted to sail past in the olden days. (Courtesy of the Outer Banks History Center; Aycock Brown, photographer)

sometimes provided for tourists to be pulled in carts between the docks and the hotels. To get from one place to another was a struggle through the deep sand that seemed to permeate the entire surface of the Outer Banks.

The almost total inaccessibility and severe seclusion of the Outer Banks kept local residents out of touch with much of outside society, which meant they were largely unaffected by life beyond their domain and changed very little by external events. As a result of that separation, they held to many of the old ways and traditions, and even their language was peppered with archaic words and ways of speaking that derived from olden times, going back even to the speech of ancestors from England, Ireland, Scotland, or other European regions. The famed Outer Banks brogue that developed there was unique, and traces of it can still be found in the speech of residents there today.

It was at the turn of the twentieth century that the Outer Banks finally became widely known, and both visitors and permanent residents were attracted to the area in large numbers for the first time. This happened because two brothers traveled there from Ohio to take advantage of the open terrain and the good winds for experiments with their new so-called flying machines. Wilbur and Orville Wright came to Kitty Hawk, where they lived while testing their gliders from atop the sand dunes of Kill Devil Hills. And they did not just test gliders, for they had devised a craft that had its own gasoline-powered engine, and they believed it could lift them into the air through its own power. Few others had such confidence, but when the Wrights successfully flew it in 1903, that event was recognized around the world. People who had never heard of Kitty Hawk or Kill Devil Hills rushed to try to get there to see where mankind's first powered flight took place. It put the Outer Banks on everyone's map.

Despite the fact that the Outer Banks now led the world in the most modern form of transportation, it was not a place where moving from one place to another was easy or, in some cases, even feasible. It was not only a place composed of sand but of *shifting* sand, and it was lucky for the Wright brothers that their contraption moved primarily above the ground.

Yet there were early towns on the Outer Banks, and travel between them was often necessary. Residents had to move to and from their homes, too, and none of it was easy or fast. Wild ponies lived on the Banks, and they were sometimes tamed and used to carry people about, but that was mostly just riding since the diminutive horses were hardly capable of pulling a heavy cart through the deep, clinging sands. Oxen had the bulk and strength to do that, though, and they were

One of the best ways to get around on the Outer Banks before the paved highway existed was aboard an oxcart, even for women dressed in their best finery. (Courtesy of the Outer Banks History Center, D. Victor Meekins Collection)

the prime cart pullers of the day. But even then, special rims were required to keep the wheels from sinking too deeply into the sand.

From frequent passage by walking or moving about by cart, clear paths eventually developed along open areas and through dense growth of what was known on the Banks as "Beach bushes." Even along those improvised pathways, sand did not compress well, and getting about still required trudging tediously through sandy trails as one's feet sometimes sank into the ground up to the ankles. Carts pulled along the rugged roadways by sturdy oxen left deep ruts, marking the way and temporarily showing their tedious route until the stirring winds erased them to leave a deceptively calm surface once more. No corduroy (log) roads were built there, but sometimes boards were laid along frequently traveled passageways to help movement. If a travel route had to cross a large, deep rift or hollow, a temporary bridge sometimes would be built to avoid the steep descent and ascent

A local Nags Head farmer hauls his watermelons to town for sale with a horse and cart. Note the wide metal tires that helped prevent the wheels from sinking into the sand. (Courtesy of the Outer Banks History Center, David Stick Collection)

needed to get across. It was difficult enough to move about on level ground. Moving on the beach was easier, but most of the towns and houses were on the sound side of the Banks — the side away from the beach. Their location was intended to avoid storms, not to facilitate mobility.

The Outer Banks were not a place visitors could reach easily, since that required a ride aboard a boat for a distance of two miles or more. And after the boat ride, movement about the Banks was clearly not simple. Even when automobiles began to arrive, travelers were left to their own ingenuity to devise a way to get about the place, requiring much resourcefulness. There were no dune buggies then, and boats only crossed water, not sand. Despite their newly found fame and popularity, the Outer Banks were still a land apart. Certain things would have to change, including access and mobility, but when those were transformed, many other things would be modified as well.

The lack of access stifled population growth on the Outer Banks, as it had done for centuries. It also stymied the plans of tourists who surged to the area with excitement about visiting and exploring the unique locale, with its recent prominence as the home of mankind's first flight. Boats continued to ply the narrow sounds between Elizabeth City or Roanoke Island and the Nags Head area, but they could never handle more than a few people, and it was apparent that a new means of entry and movement must be found if travel to and on the Banks was to become routine. Locals sought to have a road built from Virginia to reach down the narrow spit that connected to the northern Banks. Such a highway could provide the needed entry, but neither of the two states seemed interested in building it, and no private investors came forth with funds for the idea. A second plan was to build a bridge from nearby Roanoke Island and also construct a road for travelers to use once they were on the Banks. North Carolina showed little enthusiasm for such a project, seemingly uninterested in supplying a means of travel to the remote spot. It was as if a moat surrounded the Outer Banks, choking off both entry and exit. No one understood the isolation of the area better than local residents, and it was the Outer Bankers themselves who would solve the problem.

CHAPTER 2

VITAL CONNECTIONS

Early in the twentieth century, as in the centuries before, the Outer Banks of North Carolina remained cut off from virtually all access by land. As we have seen, although the barrier-island chain is connected to the southeastern edge of Virginia, there is no road onto the isolated strip of land from there, and it is bounded by water on all other sides. The only way to get to and from the Banks, or to move among their various parts, was by boat. Manteo, the largest town on Roanoke Island, became an active center of trade with Virginia and with the inland portions of North Carolina, but it is separated from Nags Head by a small body of water called Roanoke Sound. The small sound, miniscule in comparison with nearby sounds, is shallow and only a couple of miles wide at its most narrow point, but it is still wide enough to prevent easy passage. Many residents of the Outer Banks owned boats and traveled to Manteo, but few visitors made their way from Roanoke Island to the outlying Banks.

Small changes had touched the Outer Banks in the nineteenth century, but it was during the next 100 years that modifications took place that revolutionized life there and brought unimagined numbers of outsiders to their shores. The invention of the automobile redefined travel everywhere, including on the Outer Banks, but at least three decades elapsed following its introduction before a significant number of cars appeared on North Carolina's barrier islands. Without a bridge spanning the sounds or paved roads on the Banks, getting

This is the kind of road that most travelers faced at Nags Head before the Virginia Dare Trail was paved in the 1930s. (Courtesy of the Outer Banks History Center, David Stick Collection)

there in an automobile and moving about was extremely difficult. Some drivers paid local entrepreneurs to carry their cars
across the sounds on improvised ferries. The ferry operations
were cobbled together by local fishermen who towed barges
behind their boats, but they operated on uncertain schedules
and only carried a couple of vehicles at a time. North Carolina
did not own or operate ferries in those years, but the home-
made versions transported vehicles from Manteo or the Elizabeth City area to the remote Banks. The cars and drivers were
dropped off on the sandy, roadless strand to fend for themselves, and with luck, they returned to the landing later to be
carried back to the mainland.

The lack of adequate means of travel to and from the Banks
was not due to insufficient interest by those who lived there.
Through the years, various groups from Dare County made

numerous pleas to the North Carolina Highway Commission for a bridge between the Nags Head area and Roanoke Island. A bridge there would greatly improve trade and travel between the mainland and the Outer Banks, but all requests were denied.

Highway Commission members could hardly be blamed for their intransigence. There seemed to be little value in building a bridge to a barely populated strip of land that stretched along almost deserted beaches for more than a hundred miles at some distance from the mainland. The Banks themselves were a bare, sandy expanse that was hard to navigate even in carts pulled by oxen, and the group responsible for the state's highways showed little interest in paving a road on a narrow band of unstable, seemingly bottomless sand disrupted in places by inlets more than a mile wide, and where storms sent waves crashing over the dunes with disturbing regularity. Few voters lived on the Banks, so the locals had negligible political sway. It is easy to understand why the commission denied the requests for a bridge to eliminate the area's almost complete isolation.

Even before the Great Depression, economic hardship struck the Outer Banks. By 1925 the great oyster beds of Dare County had been overharvested, leaving them bleak and unproductive. Commercial fishing had also declined measurably during the period, and erosion wiped out many of the lush, grassy areas until they were no longer suitable for raising livestock. Federal control of wildlife impacted hunt clubs so that market hunters and sportsmen no longer found it worthwhile to go to the Banks. Even salvaging wrecked ships, once a windfall for natives, became a rarity after steam replaced sail and few ships ended up stranded on the shores.

The Roanoke Sound Bridge

By 1926 Washington Franklin Baum, chairman of the Dare County Board of Commissioners, concluded that something had to be done to save the population of the Outer Banks and rescue its economy. He and commissioners E. D. Midgett, R. E. Burrus, M. V. Hooper, and A. J. Fulcher foresaw that bridging Roanoke Sound would enhance travel between Nags Head and Roanoke Island, improving trade and increasing income for residents. Baum journeyed to Raleigh to make the case for the Outer Banks and try once more to convince state leaders of the need for a bridge. The state refused again, however, telling him he might as well go back home since it would be fifty years before there would be any bridges over the sounds or any roads on the Banks.

Baum and the Dare County commissioners were not dissuaded by the lack of cooperation by North Carolina officials, and, demonstrating the independent spirit for which the Bankers were known, they began to make their own plans for eliminating the gap between the Outer Banks and the outside world. If a bridge were to be built across Roanoke Sound between Nags Head and Roanoke Island, the Outer Bankers would have to supply the funding themselves. The commissioners decided to get money for the project by passing a bond issue in the county. The problem was that total property evaluation for Dare County was only around $2.5 million, hardly enough to fund construction at the 10 percent rate allowed on property valuations. But with the help of Mathias D. Hayman, their local representative in the North Carolina legislature, they were able to exceed this limit and pass a local bond issue for the needed amount of $300,000.

Now that the commissioners had the necessary financial support, they were ready to start work. Detractors added new obstacles by complaining that the bridge would only be used by Roanoke Islanders to reach the beach, making the effort a waste of money. Business owners in Manteo who feared the effects of competition also denounced the project. But Baum, who had faced the negativity of leaders in Raleigh and overcome financial obstacles, was not to be dissuaded by local malcontents lacking imagination. The majority of voters in the county had passed the issue, the money was there, and, as Baum and the commissioners saw it, so was the need.

Before the Virginia Dare Trail was paved, some cottages were built near the beach at Nags Head. Storms later washed many of these away, but some still stand. Notice the cart tracks in the foreground. (Courtesy of the Outer Banks History Center, David Stick Collection)

The bridge would need to span a gap of around two miles, but a ridge of sand along the perimeter of the marsh would allow a causeway to cover much of that distance, reducing the length of the bridge to just a mile. An abandoned roadbed on Roanoke Island was adapted as an approach to the bridge, allowing a savings of several thousand dollars.

When construction began, carpenters assembled a wooden trestle-style bridge using eighteen-foot timbers four inches thick and a foot wide. They placed the structure atop creosoted pilings forty feet long that were driven eighteen feet deep into the marshy base. The span offered a twenty-two-foot-high passageway underneath, enough for most boats, but a draw section was needed for vessels with higher superstructures. Builders purchased an old abandoned railway bridge for $1,000, towed it into the sound, and secured it into place for that purpose. Construction took less than two years from initial dredging to the first automobile crossing in late 1927.

The Roanoke Sound Bridge, with its roadway a narrow sixteen feet across, was a flimsy structure by modern standards, but it was a doorway to the future for the Outer Banks and an amazing accomplishment by the Dare County Board of Commissioners. Even Washington Baum likely did not realize the full impact the bridge would have on the growth and potential for the Outer Banks. Despite starting from a dirt road on Roanoke Island and ending at Whalebone Junction—where sandy ruts led everywhere or nowhere, depending on one's driving skills—the Roanoke Sound Bridge would alter life forever on the Banks and throughout Dare County.

For the first time ever, automobiles could be driven back and forth between Roanoke Island and Nags Head, opening the Outer Banks to tourism and trade in a way never seen before. The isolation of the Outer Banks was ended once and for all—and without outside help. A toll of $1.00 per car was charged to cross the bridge, and the income was used to repay the bonds. Many drivers happily paid the toll, which was little enough for such a unique travel experience. Around 40,000 automobiles crossed the bridge in the first year alone. The onset of the Great Depression in 1929 caused a reduction in the number of visitors to the Banks, but when the North Carolina Highway Commission bought the bridge for $135,000 in 1935, taking it over and eliminating the toll charges, only $15,000 remained to be paid off on the bonds that had been issued less than a decade earlier.

The North Carolina Highway Commission began building a new bridge in 1950 just a few feet away from the original wooden bridge, which had deteriorated from the weather and from a quarter century of transit by thousands of automobiles. Its one-foot boards had warped until they clattered loosely and loudly as drivers tried to cross, causing some trepidation over the passage.

The replacement bridge, which opened in 1952, was six feet wider than the old span and built of more durable con-

Whales were once hunted from the Outer Banks, and they still wash up occasionally and become stranded on the shore. (Courtesy of the Outer Banks History Center, Drew Wilson Collection)

crete. The new structure was still called the Roanoke Sound Bridge, but it was renamed the Washington F. Baum Bridge in 1962 in recognition of the forethought and resolve of its founder. Baum, in his eighties at the renaming, richly deserved the honor. In his book *The Outer Banks of North Carolina*, Outer Banks resident and local historian David Stick noted of Baum's extraordinary contribution: "In the long history of Dare County, the one most important event, insofar as the future of Dare County was concerned, was the construction of the Roanoke Sound Bridge. And the individual, by his foresight, determination and tenacity in the face of widespread opposition and criticism, who had nonetheless made the greatest contribution to the county, was Wash Baum."

In 1990 a modern concrete-and-steel structure costing $15.3 million replaced the second bridge. U.S. representative Walter B. Jones helped find federal funding, so North

Carolina only had to pay one-fifth of the total cost, or a little more than $3 million. The price was a good investment for the state and continued the legacy of that great bridge, which still serves as a popular route for travel to and from the Outer Banks today.

A Bridge across Currituck Sound

The building of the Roanoke Sound Bridge and its replacements changed the future and fortune of the Outer Banks in innumerable ways, one of which was by serving as the catalyst for the later construction of North Carolina Highway 12. Surprisingly, however, within five years of the completion of that bridge, and again without any state support, another bridge was put into place that brought the Outer Banks in range of the mainland. In 1928 a group of businessmen in Elizabeth City, North Carolina, a town located just northwest of Roanoke Island on the other side of Albemarle Sound, saw the opportunity to develop and sell beach properties on the Outer Banks now that traveling there by automobile was possible. They decided to buy Outer Banks beach property as an investment and planned a purchase of a seven-mile strip of the Banks in the Kitty Hawk region north of Nags Head. The area would be divided into lots and sold.

The financiers knew prospective buyers could cross the new Roanoke Sound Bridge to get to the Banks, but more than ten miles of treacherous sands faced drivers between southern Nags Head and the lots near Kitty Hawk, and that might discourage buyers. Highways to Elizabeth City from Virginia and other states might bring customers, but they could not easily reach Roanoke Island nor the development area on the Banks. As a result, the group decided to build their own bridge to connect Elizabeth City with Kitty Hawk. Noting the apparent ease with which the Dare commissioners had built their bridge, the businessmen decided they could do just as well, despite the fact that the point-to-point crossing of Currituck Sound was three miles long rather than just two.

The investment group, initially called the Currituck-Dare Bridge Company, was headed by L. C. Blades as president, Sam B. Parker as secretary, and W. G. Gaither as treasurer, all of Elizabeth City. They were later joined by Charles W. Harrison, formerly of Elizabeth City but then living in New York. The group bought nearly 6,000 acres at Kitty Hawk, divided the tract into lots, and prepared to sell them once the bridge was in place. The bridge would be paid for through the sale of stock, as well as through loans and credit.

Construction began in 1929. The bridge would depart from Point Harbor, a few miles south of Elizabeth City, cross Currituck Sound, and arrive at Martin's Point at Kitty Hawk. Problems arose early, for, after a half mile of pilings were in place and grading of a right-of-way started at Kitty Hawk, the stock market crashed. The financial collapse brought plans for the bridge tumbling down as well. Harrison abandoned the plan and departed the group, but some of those who remained decided to go ahead with the project regardless of the status of the stock market. Renaming their organization the Wright Memorial Bridge Company, and relying on more loans and credit, the little group acquired the support of supervising engineer George C. Dodge and the W. L. Jones Construction Company and went ahead with the building of the bridge.

The bridge project met some financial obstacles, but it was still completed in less than a year and opened for business on September 27, 1930. Like its southern neighbor crossing Roanoke Sound, the Currituck bridge cost $1.00 per car and driver to cross, plus an extra twenty-five cents for each additional passenger. The successful builders named their project the Wright Memorial Bridge, capitalizing on the recent national publicity for the building of a memorial on the Outer Banks honoring the Wright brothers' first flight. The bridge was almost three miles long and was also a drawbridge, allowing ships with high masts to pass underneath. A large iron archway greeted travelers at the entrance to the Banks on the bridge, proudly announcing that it led the way to Dare County, the birthplace of the nation in 1584 and of aviation

The U.S. Lifesaving Service carried their boats to the surf on carts drawn by horses, which, along with oxen, pulled carts all over the Outer Banks. (Courtesy of the Outer Banks History Center, Dare County Tourist Bureau Collection)

in 1903. The bridge was a bold and successful venture by insightful planners, a bonus to the Outer Banks, and a credit to the little organization from Elizabeth City, but the beach development project would not turn out to be as profitable for those investors as they might have hoped.

North Carolina Takes Over

During the Depression, the economy declined across the nation, including in North Carolina, where few visitors were interested in buying Kitty Hawk property. Income from tolls to cross the Wright Memorial Bridge diminished, and the Kitty Hawk developers began to encounter financial difficulties. Mortgage holders and lenders with liens against the property of the Wright Memorial Bridge Company were compassionate and extended their dates of foreclosure beyond the

Stumps of old forests show how the Atlantic Ocean has encroached through the years at the northern end of the Banks. Westward migration of the barrier islands is not just a recent phenomenon. (Courtesy of the Outer Banks History Center, Aycock Brown Collection)

times originally set, but this could not go on indefinitely. As if things were not bad enough, in 1933 the North Carolina legislature made the decision to buy both the Wright Memorial Bridge and the Roanoke Sound Bridge and eliminate the tolls entirely. State leaders might have been somewhat embarrassed watching the success of the local bridge-building groups after they themselves had refused to act, but now that the bridges were in place, they were ready to correct their mistake and intended to take possession and control.

The Wright Memorial Bridge Company stockholders saw dim prospects for the future and tried to salvage their project. They sought unsuccessfully to have county taxes reduced on their Kitty Hawk landholdings to cut the serious drain those fees imposed on their income. In August 1933, despite their desperate efforts, they were forced to sell their remaining development land on the Outer Banks for a mere $20,000 when First Citizens National Bank of Elizabeth City foreclosed on it.

North Carolina's plans to buy the bridge might have still allowed the stockholders of the Wright Memorial Bridge Company and its associated properties to avoid loss, but the state offered to pay only $150,000. The original indebtedness for the construction was $300,000 and the amount still owed was greater than the suggested purchase price, so the group balked at first and refused to sell. The state then declared it would build a parallel bridge beside the existing one and offer passage without any tolls. That clearly would be the death knell for the original bridge, and the owners would not even receive $150,000 the state was offering. As a result, on June 20, 1935, the voting stockholders elected to sell at the stated price. North Carolina now owned both bridges over the sounds to the Outer Banks.

The builders of the Wright Memorial Bridge, who achieved a worthy goal despite the failure of the Outer Banks development project, lost their money—although state leaders did the right thing by removing the tolls at a time when the economies of North Carolina and the rest of the nation were suffering. The organizers of the Wright Memorial Bridge Company suffered a loss, but they added significantly to the growth of the Outer Banks, which now had two roadways connecting them with the rest of the world.

The Wright Memorial Bridge has remained in operation for many years. North Carolina repaired it in 1938 after it was heavily damaged by ice floes during an unusually severe winter, and the state rebuilt it entirely in the 1940s despite numerous delays caused by World War II. Ice chunks damaged it again in 1958, and it had to be repaired once more. The bridge was replaced by a more substantial concrete structure in 1966. T. A. Loving Company began building the replacement in July 1964 and cast the final section in May 1966. The 2.8-mile span cost $3.3 million, more than ten times the cost of the original bridge and more than the total property valuation for all of Dare County forty years earlier. The older bridge continued to function right to the end, as traffic flowed across it over Currituck Sound while its concrete replacement was being built parallel to it just eighty feet to the south.

In only a decade, the Outer Banks had gone from having no connections over the sounds to having two bridges for residents and visitors to move to and from the shores of North Carolina's outlying barrier-island chain. Local newspapers like the *Virginian-Pilot* and the *Coastland Times* offer numerous contemporary stories for those who wish to discover more about the actual construction of the two bridges, and to see how the ambition and determination of two different groups of Outer Banks advocates—supported somewhat reluctantly by the state of North Carolina—had led to these great achievements so much sooner than the fifty years once predicted. Life on the Outer Banks would never be the same.

CHAPTER

3

A NEW ERA DAWNS FOR
THE OUTER BANKS

Private developers succeeded where the state had been too jittery or obstinate to act, and completion of two bridges over the sounds made it possible for significant numbers of travelers to get onto and off of the Outer Banks for the first time. Increased traffic flow promised to stimulate commerce, but when vehicles began to cross the sounds to the northern Banks after the bridges opened, drivers found the going difficult. Travelers spun their wheels in frustration as they ground their way through the sand, for there were no roads suitable for cars on the Outer Banks. Only the sprawling tracks from earlier arrivals marked the way, and sometimes the parallel, winding ruts still had cars imbedded in them. Driving across the shifting, loose, grainy surface of the Outer Banks was daunting and definitely not for the faint of heart.

After automobiles made their appearance in America, but before bridges spanned the sounds, a few fortunate, or perhaps unfortunate, residents of the Outer Banks acquired cars for their own transport, and early visitors who dared to bring their vehicles over on ferries added to the small number of cars lumbering around on the roadless Banks. Whether leaving the docks or the yards of local owners, automobiles had to be maneuvered with improvisation and skill, for the environment was unforgiving. Moving over the soft, sugary sand was a problem for both car and driver, loose-grained grit permeated everything, and salty air coated metal surfaces

One of the early boats that carried visitors between Roanoke Island and Nags Head was the *Hattie Creef*. It was a popular means of travel before the Washington Baum and Wright Memorial Bridges were built. (Courtesy of the Outer Banks History Center, Town Collection)

with rust. Heavy vehicles often sank until sometimes their chassis rested on top of the sand in what was known locally as "bottoming out," leaving the wheels to spin uselessly. Drivers' patience, like the rubber and metal of the cars, was eroded quickly, and some vehicles were abandoned to become permanent captives—much like the scattered wreckage of ships already buried around the islands, mute testimony to the hazards of the area. But automobiles on the Outer Banks were symbolic of a new day.

David Stick has described the creativity among early drivers that enabled some movement about the Banks despite the ubiquitous sand that clutched at rubber tires with tenacity and grim determination. Mechanized travel, it was discovered, was possible between the high- and low-tide zones. The wrack line at the highest reach of the waves marked the border of a broad avenue where wet sand was pounded flat by the surf for miles along the open beach. It was almost like a paved highway, and cars whizzed along the edge of the surf at a fair speed, although the loose, malleable sand higher up would trap them in an instant. Semipermanent ruts did evolve on the higher ground, usually following common lanes of travel between towns, and such pathways were sometimes lined with boards, making them more suitable for travel. There were no asphalt highways, but the improvised roadways were better than nothing.

Ben Dixon MacNeill, a local resident and author, claimed in his book *The Hatterasman* that in 1938 he drove the thirty-eight miles between the Cape Hatteras Lighthouse and Oregon Inlet in only thirty-two minutes along the hard-packed sand of the beach. He admitted it might have been foolish, but he said the idea was infectious. "Here a reasonably efficient vehicle in good running order," he stated in his book, "and here a road, a hundred yards wide and as smooth as pavement. Why not?"

Necessity and experience taught drivers to carry shovels for digging, pry bars for lifting, sacking for traction, and perhaps a couple of passengers for pushing. The early oxcarts on the Banks used wide rims that were twice the normal size to keep the wheels from sinking, and motorists learned to deflate their tires slightly so the flattened tires would offer a wider footprint and greater support on sandy surfaces. Local residents called early automobile tires "balloon" tires, for they held soft rubber inner tubes that could be deflated and then reinflated with a hand-operated air pump, allowing better traction when needed.

Primitive forms of automobile travel evolved on the Banks in the second and third decades of the twentieth century, and the design of early cars was also helpful. The Ford Model T and Model A had high undercarriages, were fitted with large-diameter wheels, used balloon tires, and were light enough to be pushed if necessary (and it usually was). There were no commercial tow trucks on the Banks in those years, but members of the local Coast Guard helped unlucky drivers stranded within sight of their stations. Rescuing drivers stuck in the sand became as common as saving sailors marooned at sea.

Surprisingly, a local bus service was established on Hatteras Island even before any roads were paved. Residents who wanted to travel along the Banks or get to the ferry docks needed a means other than walking or riding a slow-moving oxcart to reach their destination. The local Midgett family, noted for their work with the U.S. Lifesaving Service, chose to meet that need by providing a bus for residents to ride in 1938. Starting with a small Ford bus, the Midgett brothers, Henderson, Anderson, and Stockton, opened the business and traveled a daily schedule between the ferry landings at Hatteras Inlet and Oregon Inlet, about fifty miles apart. The buses stopped at towns in between to pick up or drop off passengers, and the earliest buses were small enough to be carried to Roanoke Island and back aboard the ferry. If driving a car on the Banks was a challenge, maneuvering a heavy bus on the sand must have been even worse. Yet, as the bus drivers gained experience, they were able to run the routes with very few failures. Rides were punctuated with excitement and occasional episodes of anxiety for both drivers and passengers, but the buses continued to roll, at least most of the time. They were a welcome mode of transportation in an era when few Bankers had cars and not many of those that did elected to drive on the treacherous sands.

The First Outer Banks Road

The North Carolina Highway Commission made a decision in 1931, shortly after the Wright Memorial Bridge was completed, to pave a highway between the ends of the two bridges at Whalebone Junction and Kitty Hawk. The paved road would run from the Wright Memorial Bridge to Point Harbor, then continue southward past Kitty Hawk and Nags Head and on to Whalebone Junction. The finished road covered eighteen miles, allowing easy travel for locals and visitors

Wealthy visitors crossed the sounds to Nags Head almost every weekend aboard boats. Most walked to the nearby hotels from the landings, but carts could provide rides along the tracks that can be seen on the pier. (Courtesy of the Outer Banks History Center, David Stick Collection)

and improving the economic growth of the area. Called the Virginia Dare Trail—said to have been named so by Frank Stick, David's father—the new road commemorated the first European child born there so many years before. The highway marked the beginning of a beach road that would someday link the Outer Banks from end to end. When North Carolina finally got control of the two bridges over the sounds, the paved road already ran between them. It is unclear whether state officials knew they would ultimately buy the two bridges when they made the move to pave the highway.

The North Carolina Highway Commission probably never imagined the short roadway would eventually extend northward to Corolla near the Virginia border and all the way to the southern tip of Ocracoke Island, but such a thoroughfare had been the dream of those who lived on the Outer Banks for years. Some of the more hopeful of the locals foresaw a highway that would stretch from Virginia Beach down the Outer Banks, run back across to the mainland and through the North Carolina beaches, and continue all the way to Myrtle Beach, South Carolina. The Highway Commission probably envisioned a remote, sandy strip that was unlikely to get any more roads for decades. Neither group was right, but a highway that ran for the entire length of the Outer Banks would end the isolation that stymied both residents and visitors and open the region to travel and development in ways that could hardly have been imagined. Arriving by boat was no longer the only way visitors could get to the Outer Banks, for the sounds were bridged and road paving had begun. Those changes would alter the nature of the Outer Banks completely and irrevocably.

Paving the short eighteen miles of road on the Outer Banks had been accomplished late and with some hesitation, but further development of a highway on the outlying areas was even more halting and uncertain. Because the first few paved miles were on the northern Banks, it was natural to expect expansion of the roadway to grow from there. Residents of the small village of Duck, located about sixteen miles north of Nags Head, believed so and were hopeful the road would soon extend their way. They wanted the road paved to Duck as soon as possible, for after leaving the Nags Head area, they had to drive in sandy ruts or along the wash of the beach to reach their homes. Their numbers were few, and the North Carolina government had little sympathy for their dilemma, so their pleas were in vain. It would be more than twenty years before the road reached Duck, just twelve miles from the northern tip of the Virginia Dare Trail.

World War II began not long after the paving of the new road, and the war effort put a halt to most development on the Outer Banks, including a highway to Duck or anywhere else. Travel continued to be difficult once drivers left the Virginia Dare Trail. Just how difficult can be seen in the following story from an early issue of *Coastland Times* in which

Before NC 12 was paved on Hatteras Island, paths and improvised roadways were scattered throughout the towns there, as can be seen in this early view of Rodanthe. (Courtesy of the Outer Banks History Center, Aycock Brown Collection)

resident Stanley Wahab describes the struggles he encountered on a trip with his daughter as they returned to the Outer Banks from Maryland.

On December 23, 1944, I drove from Baltimore, Maryland, to Ocracoke, North Carolina, which is now the southernmost end of Cape Hatteras National Seashore Park. Driving was good and uneventful until arriving at Whalebone, about three miles south of Nags Head where the hard surface road terminated. Stopping at Mrs. Neva Midgett's Service Station to deflate the tires on my Buick to fifteen pounds air pressure, I was advised not to attempt to drive farther as five automobiles had been stuck before getting to Oregon Inlet. However, being a "Banker" with some experience in sand driving and with more time than money, I started driving. The beach between Whalebone and Oregon Inlet was flooded from a heavy rainfall. Motor quit about one mile from Bodie Island Coast Guard Station to which I waded for assistance, which was promptly rendered, and I proceeded to the 8-car ferry which landed on the south point of Oregon Inlet. I knew it would be futile to attempt to drive through the sand inside of the beach wash. Fortunately, the tide was at low ebb so I could drive along the wash of the surf. Everything went well until about two miles from the Cape Hatteras Coast Guard Station, when I ran into a bed of gravel sand, lost two hub caps and was stuck. I found a net stake on which I tied a kimono belonging to my daughter who was along with me, placed this on top of the highest hill as a signal for assistance to the Cape Hatteras Coast Guard Station. The wind was blowing from the SW, the atmosphere was hazy which made very little visibility. After waiting more than an hour, it was nearly dark without any response to our improvised signal. The tide was rising and water washing under my automobile. We decided it was time to adopt other means of attracting attention of the Coast Guard.

The beach in this vicinity was strewn with wreckage and debris from ships which had been torpedoed and sunk by the Germans. We picked up pieces of wreckage and piled on top of the hill where our signal was still flying unheeded. Being aware of the fact that the Coast Guard was constantly on the alert for the sight of fire, I said to Lilian my daughter, "This will bring 'em." We only had three matches left. The wind blew my first and second matches out in an attempt to set fire to the wood pile, so I decided to replenish with more newspapers. The fire started on the third match and so did the Coast Guard with their Power Wagon and a jeep reaching us in short order and towing us to Hatteras.

I related this as being one of the milder trips I have rode along the banks during the past fifty years. I have walked many miles, ridden horseback, hitchhiked and recall one ride in an ox cart.

Stanley Wahab was the president of the All Seashore Highway Association, whose goal was a roadway that stretched from Virginia to South Carolina. He and other members of the association advocated a road that would open all the beaches of those states to easy travel. He understood that more paved highway on the Outer Banks would form a major component of the association's plan. His experience during his trip must have added to his determination to build such a road.

The Hatteras Island Road

When World War II ended, the notion of paving more roads on the Banks arose again, but it was not Duck and the northern Banks that were added to a hard-surfaced Outer Banks road. Rather, it was Hatteras Island, the middle section of the Outer Banks. Growth of fishing activities near Cape Hatteras, both as a sport and as a business, took a sudden upturn right after the war, leading to additional traffic arriving at Hatteras Village from the mainland. Professional fishermen working out of Hatteras docks needed to transport their catch to the mainland for sale, and sport fishermen eager to reach the prime fishing locations on Hatteras Island also clamored for better access. Hatteras Island posed the same problems for drivers that had confounded others on the Outer Banks for years. A paved road was needed, and pressure to build a highway there expanded along with the increase in fishing activities.

A 1944 North Carolina Highway Department map shows a dotted line stretching from one end of Hatteras Island to the other, and a key to the symbols on the map indicates the broken line represents a primitive road. There was no paved highway, nor even a graded, drained dirt road on the island

Boats, horses, and carts were the means of transportation on the Outer Banks at the turn of the twentieth century. These were at Chicamacomico in 1899. (Courtesy of the Outer Banks History Center, Carol Cronkcole Collection)

at the time, and those who tried to travel along the route indicated by the dotted line probably felt that "primitive" was too kind a word, if not downright flattering.

A paved highway would certainly enhance travel and boost business on the long, narrow island, but not all Hatteras residents were in favor of such a road. They figured its existence would end their secluded status and cause expansion and development of the kind seen around Nags Head. So they protested the idea, although it turned out they need not have worried: the rampant growth that had changed the northern Banks would not occur on Hatteras Island when it finally got its highway.

A delegation of local representatives left Hatteras Island to visit Governor Robert Cherry in Raleigh, presenting him with a gift of shad and telling him of the readily available supply of fish they could provide if only they had a road to move it. The governor must have been influenced by the mission and the gift, for he decided to go to Hatteras Island and check out the situation himself. As soon as his vehicle landed on the island, it promptly became stuck, and the governor himself had to push to help extricate it. Prompted by his findings, and perhaps by getting stuck, Governor Cherry decided Hatteras Island really did need a hard-surfaced road, so in 1947 North Carolina paved a twelve-mile stretch starting at Hatteras Village and extending northward almost to Avon.

The new road connected three of the seven diminutive villages between Cape Hatteras and Oregon Inlet, so when that road opened in 1948, Hatteras, Frisco, and Buxton were all linked by a paved highway. But less than a third of the length of Hatteras Island was accessible by the new paved road, and twenty-nine miles of unpaved travel still lay between the Oregon Inlet ferry landing and the end of the new road just south of Avon. The pavement also began one mile inland from the ferry landing at Hatteras Inlet, and drivers had to struggle to cross the open sand to reach the road after they disembarked the ferry.

Not much happened to improve travel along any segment of the Outer Banks for the next couple of years, other than ongoing maintenance of existing roads. But when Kerr Scott became the governor of North Carolina in 1949, he came into office on a promise of providing paved roads for the majority of people in the state. His ambitious road-building initiative impacted many of the rural areas of North Carolina, and that included the Outer Banks. Most of the isolated sites along the Banks were connected during his term in office, and many of the needed segments of what would become the long-sought Beach Road were begun under his administration.

The first Outer Banks road project stemming from Governor Scott's leadership was the construction of another seventeen miles of paved highway from the end of the Hatteras road south of Avon northward to the town of Rodanthe near the lower tip of Pea Island National Wildlife Refuge. That paving was completed by 1951, but a temporary halt was put on construction until an argument could be settled regarding the best way to continue. The last dozen miles of roadway to Oregon Inlet would pass through the wildlife refuge, and a way had to be devised to allow this to happen without disturbing the birds or other wildlife. Paving the final twelve miles on Hatteras Island would have to wait. The U.S. Fish and Wildlife Service, in charge of the Pea Island Refuge, asked that a barbed-wire fence be built on both sides of the road if it were extended to Oregon Inlet. The barrier would keep cars and people from trespassing into the refuge areas as they traveled the highway. Wildlife Service officials feared the gathering and nesting of birds in the refuge would be disrupted if too many visitors moved unfettered across the protected zones. Highway officials were not convinced of the need for a fence and were worried that costs for the right-of-way and the protective barricade could run as high a $25,000, so they stalled in uncertainty for a year. The Dare County Board of Commissioners, desperate to get the road finished, made an appeal for the highway to be paved through the refuge without further ado, and the North Carolina Highway Commission made a bid to the U.S. Congress for help. A bill was quickly introduced into the House of Representatives to permit the continuance of the paving regardless of right-of-way considerations and without the installation of a fence. The bill was passed by Congress, clearing the way for the road to be finished.

Even before the last piece of roadway was paved on Pea Island, as many as 100 vehicles a day were traversing the sandy trail from the Oregon Inlet ferry landing to Rodanthe. It was a treacherous pathway of dips, gullies, and water-filled potholes, interrupted midway by flooded zones along the former channel of New Inlet, where cars were likely to become stuck or have their engines drown out. It was worse when the tide was in. A great deal of pushing and digging was needed to remove stuck vehicles from their predicaments; it is hard to imagine that travel along a paved highway would be more disturbing than that to the bird population of the refuge.

An agreement was reached that the road could be paved across the refuge, and the job was completed in 1953. The one-mile rift between the road's end at the town of Hatteras and the Hatteras Inlet ferry dock was also paved that year,

Diminutive early post offices, which often gave new names to Outer Banks towns, were accessible by boat, oxcart, and sometimes automobiles, as can be seen by the sandy ruts leading by this one in Avon. (Courtesy of the Outer Banks History Center, Aycock Brown Collection)

providing a continuous roadway that linked the ferry landing at Oregon Inlet with the ferry landing at Hatteras Inlet. Paved highway now ran the entire length of Hatteras Island, the longest part of the Outer Banks barrier-island chain, putting it ahead of the northern Banks despite their earlier start. The new Hatteras Island highway was named North Carolina State Road 1001, a title it would keep until 1963.

The North Carolina Highway Commission was not the only group that paved roads on the Outer Banks during that era. In 1952 the U.S. National Park Service paved five miles of highway from the Virginia Dare Trail at Whalebone Junction to the vicinity of the Bodie Island Lighthouse on Bodie Island. They paved a parking lot at the lighthouse as well.

The state then paved three additional miles from the end of the national park road all the way to Oregon Inlet and called that short road SR 1001, tying its label to the road on Hatteras Island. It was now possible to drive on a hard-surface road from either the Wright Memorial Bridge or the Roanoke Island Bridge all the way to Oregon Inlet.

The new road on Hatteras Island made driving simpler, and even the Midgett's Manteo-Hatteras buses took two hours instead of the usual six to get from one end of the island to the other. The ease of passage on the new road dramatically increased the number of visitors as well.

Not everything went well with the new road on Hatteras Island, however, for the increased number of visitors quickly overwhelmed the capacity of the free ferry at Oregon Inlet. Traffic jams and long waits greeted travelers trying to cross the inlet, especially in the summer. Other, more serious problems developed on Hatteras Island itself. Until then, drivers had been left to their own discretion while operating their motor vehicles on the island, and many had done so without regard to the rules of the road since there had been no road. And because a driver's license was not required, no driver's license office had been opened there, and the North Carolina State Highway Patrol had no local representation. With a paved highway in place, certain guidelines of safety had to be considered and the old ways had to go. This soon became painfully apparent. Within a year of the road being paved, several fatal auto accidents occurred on Hatteras Island. People learned quickly that they could not leave their vehicles parked in the roadway—especially with no lights on at night, when other cars were likely to come along moving at a high rate of speed. And though it had become easy to drive fast, doing so was not advisable when other drivers were present on the road, which was narrow and allowed little room for miscalculation.

The accident rate, especially those with fatalities, got everyone's attention and caused North Carolina to assign a highway patrolman to Hatteras Island in 1957. Residents welcomed

Before paved roads came to the Outer Banks, makeshift dirt roads me-andered through the region. (Courtesy of the Outer Banks History Center, Aycock Brown Collection)

him, for he quickly reined in dangerous drivers. Those who carelessly raced up and down the new roadway and engaged in other risky driving habits were hauled into court, where their fines persuaded them to desist from those hazardous activities. The state also opened a license examiner's office at Avon in the summer of 1957, a facility that would serve both Hatteras Island and Ocracoke Island. Sibyl Etheridge of Manteo, who had operated a part-time office for driver's licensing on Roanoke Island, was given additional responsi-bility for Hatteras and Ocracoke Islands, where for the first time a license was required to drive. The new law officers soon took charge of enforcing the legal statutes on the island road in the same manner that they were enforced elsewhere in the state. The road became much safer for drivers, their passengers, and their cars. Hatteras Island now had an official highway and no longer just a dotted line on a map.

Construction of the paved highway on Hatteras Island was completed at an opportune time since Cape Hatteras National Seashore, the first national seashore park in the United States, was established on the Outer Banks in 1953, and it included almost all of Hatteras Island as well as most of Ocracoke Island. A large influx of visitors came to Hatteras Island as a result of the establishment of the park, and the new road accommodated them in a way that would have been impossible before. Some Hatteras Island locals dreaded automobiles, for in the early years before the road was paved, drivers often chose to drive across grassy areas rather than on the unforgiving sand, and as a result, the grass on the island was disappearing. One man claimed that a single automobile trip down the island could destroy more grass than a cow could consume in a year. With thousands of cars pouring onto the island after the development of the national park, having a paved road for them to ride on was a very good thing. (The grass also would recover since all the cows were soon gone from the island as well.)

A Manteo-Hatteras Bus Saga

On a cold September morning in 1954, a nor'easter was blowing across Hatteras Island. Wind-driven waves slashed at the shore and rocketed across the sand and dunes in great sheets of brine and froth, immersing the beach and parts beyond in the rushing waters. Low-hanging clouds were whipped along before the storm, paralleling the direction of the waves and adding to the impression that the whole earth was moving rapidly to the west.

Moving perpendicular to this apparent shifting of the island's surface was a small, green Ford bus carrying about twenty people and driven by a young man named Stockton Midgett, who was determined to get his load of passengers safely from the town of Hatteras to Oregon Inlet despite the tempest that was attempting to engulf them. As they came within a few miles of the inlet, they rode along a new portion of highway that had just been completed from Rodanthe across Pea Island Wildlife Refuge to reach the ferry landing, where open water separated Hatteras Island from the northern portion of the Outer Banks. This final portion of pavement provided a solid roadway instead of the sandy trail that was the normal surface faced by the youthful driver. The bus had made the trip countless times as part of the operation run by the Midgett family to help travelers get to and from the northern Banks or Roanoke Island, as well as back and forth across Hatteras Island itself.

The youngest Midgett boys, Stockton and his brother Anderson, had driven the bus from the time they were big enough to see over the steering wheel, even though in their earliest years they had to sit on pillows to accomplish that— much to the consternation and concern of passengers. When they first started driving the bus, the boys were too young to get a driver's license, but that was not a problem: no license was required at the remote location, and besides, they were experienced and skilled long before they reached what would have been the required minimum age for legal permits.

Before the road was paved, the Midgett lads often transported their nervous fares along the open sand that stretched for miles along the eastern shore of Hatteras Island. Maneuvering skillfully around the dunes and gullies, they steered over the wet, packed sand at the very edge of the waves, where the steady beat of the water made the surface as unyielding as concrete. Occasionally, the wheels actually intersected the waves, flinging great splashes of salt water over the bus as it hurtled along.

The new highway presented a better way for the bus and was beyond the reach of ordinary waves, but on this day, the wave action was far from ordinary. As the bus barreled along, drenched by rain and rocked by the wind, the water from the Atlantic roiled across the highway and hid the pavement from view. As the storm intensified, the few scattered yaupon trees beside the road bent precariously before the gale, and the water grew deeper until continual echelons of battering waves surged over the road, making it difficult to stay on the hard surface or to even see where it was. Although young Stockton had made this daily run many times before, he had never tried to drive in a storm like this one. Unable to do more than guess at the margins of the highway, he peered nervously out through the windshield as the wipers struggled in vain to rake away the streaming sheets of rainfall mixed with salt water that was splashed into the bus's path by wind and wave.

The worried passengers looked fearfully out of the windows as the storm seemed about to overwhelm them and the bus. Their hands gripped the seat rails in what they would later call a knuckle-whitening clinch as the bus shook and swayed before the powerful gusts of wind that rattled them to the bone. Waves washed steadily against the wheels and threatened to push the vehicle off the road—if it was even still on it. The passengers trusted Stockton, who had a reputation as a skilled driver, but some wondered if they should offer him advice—then nervously realized they did not know what advice to give.

By now, the driver had slowed the bus until it barely crawled along, for it was impossible to see more than a few feet in front of the engine. Just ahead, the powerful, surging waves had sliced through the pavement and washed a deep channel across the highway. Stockton could not see the large washout or even the pavement itself, and before he or anyone on board could make a move to protect themselves, the bus plunged headlong over the rim of the gully and down into the murky depths until only the rear half of the Ford protruded above the surface of the flooded roadway. Soon, even that began to slide from view. Stockton guided the passengers quickly to the rear of the deeply canted bus and out the emergency door. With great haste, they jumped from the vehicle and into the swirling waters, leaving the stranded bus to sink ever deeper into the quicksand-like muck that held it captive.

By the time they were all safely out of the bus and standing in knee-deep water, only about eight inches of the little green Ford remained visible above the surface.

Men from the nearby Coast Guard station saw the accident and quickly came to the passengers' assistance. All the passengers were rescued, much to Stockton Midgett's satisfaction, for he had never lost a customer or a bus, although this time it must have seemed a very close call. The bus line had experienced prior breakdowns, and episodes of getting stuck were too numerous to count, but no mishap or incident had come this close to hurling a Midgett bus forever into the maw of Hatteras Island. The next day, after the storm had abated and the waters receded, work crews were able to dig away the sand and extract the vehicle from what could have easily become its grave—and maybe the graves of the passengers and driver as well. The company sent another bus to carry the somewhat rattled passengers on to their destination the next morning, but that ride must have seemed humdrum. Stockton himself went on to drive the bus for almost ten more years.

The account of this episode with the old Ford bus was obtained through a recent interview with Tim Midgett, the son of Stockton, the driver of the bus. Tim told stories from his memories and also shared the family scrapbook that contains numerous stories from local newspapers like the *Coastland Times* and the *Virginian-Pilot* that relate the exciting thrills of operating the bus line on early, roadless Hatteras Island.

The Manteo-Hatteras bus line continued to run successfully to and from the town of Hatteras and the other small towns that lay sprinkled along the island until 1963, when it was sold to a Virginia bus company. During its run of almost twenty-five years, it was the principal means of transportation for residents and visitors on Hatteras Island. The Midgetts claimed to have never failed to start their trips on schedule, and they only failed to complete a trip twenty times in all those years of business.

Tim, who today owns and manages a real estate business

on Hatteras Island, mentioned that the original bus station became the real estate office after the bus business was sold. It was the trips to Manteo on the bus that gave the family the opportunity to start dealing in Outer Banks real estate while waiting for the return ride on the ferry. They still serve visitors today by helping them locate places to spend their vacations on the island—but those travelers must move up and down the road without the Manteo-Hatteras bus service.

The troubles faced by bus operations on Hatteras Island were the same that early drivers endured everywhere on the Outer Banks. The Hatteras Island road was repaired after the 1954 sinking of the bus, much as it would have to be fixed many times after that when fierce storms washed the asphalt away or cut pathways across the island at its thinnest spots. The paved highway on the Outer Banks would remain in eternal conflict with the weather there, and the ultimate victor is still uncertain.

Other Road Construction

At about the time the final segments of the road on Hatteras Island were being completed, an asphalt-surfaced highway was built from the upper end of the Virginia Dare Trail toward Duck, north of Nags Head. The new pavement stretched from near the exit ramp of the Wright Memorial Bridge northward along the Banks all the way to the Currituck County line. The roadway, labeled State Road 1200, opened in 1953 and finally included the remote town of Duck, whose residents had waited two decades to get their own highway. In spite of the added mileage, the village of Corolla, just a dozen miles farther north, was left stranded in the sand of the Banks with no easy way to get between there and Duck. Not until 1987 would the final section between Duck and Corolla be added to the Outer Banks road that locals had sought for so many years.

In 1952, just before the Virginia Dare Trail was extended northward as SR 1200, minor changes were made at Whale-

Until NC 12 was extended to Corolla in the 1980s, the village was a desolate, isolated area where the Currituck Lighthouse, the Whalehead Club, and half a dozen scattered buildings were all that could be seen. Just twenty-five years later, hundreds of cottages and dozens of businesses permeated the area. (Courtesy of the Outer Banks History Center, Aycock Brown Collection)

bone Junction, and a new name was given to the part of the highway that led across the Washington F. Baum Bridge to Roanoke Island. The roadway was given the new title of US 158/64/264, but that was a complex name for a very short road and was soon abbreviated to just US 64 since it was an extension of the same US 64 that led from the mainland to Roanoke Island. That short highway carried visitors across the Washington F. Baum Bridge, while sixteen miles to the north, highway US 158 led to the Outer Banks over the Wright Memorial Bridge, and the two joined the ends of the Virginia Dare Trail.

The dream for a highway that would run along the beach and span the Outer Banks from end to end began to look like an achievable goal at last, even if it was still only a patchwork of small paved segments scattered across the islands' various parts. Except for the missing link between Corolla and Duck, one could now drive on paved road all the way down the Outer Banks to Cape Hatteras. Parts of the highway existed under different names, and a short ferry ride was required over Oregon Inlet, but it covered a good bit of the Banks. Only Ocracoke Island, south of Hatteras Island, still had no state-paved road at all.

Ocracoke Island Highway

Ocracoke Island, which lies between Cape Hatteras and Portsmouth Island, was a favorite haunt of the pirate Blackbeard and attracts many modern visitors as well. Privately operated ferries ran from Atlantic and Swan Quarter on the mainland to the southern end of Ocracoke Island after 1938. These toll routes fed tourists onto the island and into Ocracoke village, but there was no easy way to get from the village to the northern end of the island, where other ferries could take them over to Hatteras Island. Merciless terrain hindered travel up and down Ocracoke Island, compounded by several different creeks that crossed the narrow isle. Just as on Hatteras Island, an early bus service carried a few passengers between the ferry docks at the extreme ends of Ocracoke. A few locals owned cars, and ferries occasionally brought other autos in from Hatteras Island, Atlantic, or Swan Quarter, but not many dared travel the forbidding sands of Ocracoke Island.

Luther Hodges, lieutenant governor of North Carolina under Governor William B. Umstead, completed Umstead's term after that governor died in office in 1954, and he was himself elected governor of the state in 1956. It was during the Hodges administration in the late fifties that much of the final leg of coastal highway was completed. But paving the

Wild ponies grazed and roamed freely over the Outer Banks before they were confined after the establishment of NC 12. This view is near New Inlet in 1899. (Courtesy of the Outer Banks History Center, Carol Cronkcole Collection)

road from Ocracoke village to the Hatteras Inlet ferry landing, like much of the other highway construction on the Outer Banks, was done in piecemeal fashion. New pavement was laid from Ocracoke village toward the northern end of the island in 1957 but stopped before reaching the end, causing Hatteras Inlet ferries to have to enter and depart from a less-advantageous point until the final three-mile portion was paved in 1958. At that time, the ferries began to dock at the new end of the highway, which cut the time of the boat ride to Hatteras Island almost in half. Ocracoke Island finally had its road—initially labeled as State Road 1323—and that newly paved highway ran for almost the entire length of the island, connecting the ferry landings at its opposite ends.

Thus by 1960 one could traverse the entire Outer Banks by automobile, except for one little portion that left Corolla disjointed from the rest of the Banks and a couple of ferry rides that were necessary to complete the route. As Corolla became more popular, developers began to buy land in the area and divide it into lots for sale. They paved a road almost to Corolla from the end of the state road just north of Duck but gated it off so only property owners were allowed through. Corolla itself was still left without a paved highway, and the paved road through the development did not help since the residents of Corolla were not allowed to use it.

What had started a little less than thirty years earlier with eighteen miles of pavement had grown into an almost completed highway of more than a hundred miles that opened the Outer Banks to new lifestyles and visitation that many would not have believed possible, except for some hopeful local residents. But that roadway was segmented into three distinct sections like the Outer Banks themselves and was divided by two open inlets where ferry transport was required. North Carolina took major steps in the early sixties that brought it closer to realizing the dream of the long-sought Beach Road to span the Outer Banks from end to end. Just three decades after the bridging of the sounds, the birthing process of an uninterrupted North Carolina Highway 12 was nearly complete.

CHAPTER

4

MISSING LINKS

Drivers hoping to travel smoothly down the narrow Outer Banks must take into account their separation from the mainland as well as the ruptures in integrity that occur along any roadway that would follow such varying coastal terrain. Getting to the Banks over the sounds and crossing the inlets that separate parts of the barrier-island chain must be considered in any plan to drive there.

Crossing the waterways surrounding the Outer Banks, as well as those fracturing them into disjointed pieces, is a process that can only be managed by boat or bridge. Thus bridges and ferries are an important part of the Outer Banks highway, for they tie the road together where parts are missing. They carry vehicles and passengers along the Outer Banks as surely as a paved highway and are vital to any travel there.

Inlets come and go on the Outer Banks, but two major inlets were opened simultaneously by a powerful hurricane in 1846. The storm isolated the Cape Hatteras area by snipping off that section of the barrier-island chain at both ends to form an island about fifty miles long. The most critical cutoff separated the northern end of what had now become Hatteras Island from the more-populated Nags Head area. The other disruption was near Cape Hatteras, where the split divided the lower end of the strip of land to form a separate isle called Ocracoke Island. Both Hatteras and Ocracoke Islands were left isolated by the inlets, and their economies were handicapped as a result. Many who lived there appreciated the seclusion found on the two islands, for they did not want to experience the rapid commercial development that was changing the northern Banks area.

Ocracoke Island is bordered on the south by Ocracoke Inlet, which had already been there for centuries. That two-mile-wide channel separated Ocracoke from its southern neighbor, Portsmouth Island. Portsmouth Island, which was barely populated at any time in its history, later became uninhabited when residents abandoned the village of Portsmouth. Travel between Ocracoke and Portsmouth ended at that time, and the only travel from the southern tip of Ocracoke Island was to the mainland, around three dozen miles across Ocracoke Inlet and Pamlico Sound. That distance was much too far to bridge, so travel between Ocracoke Island and the mainland was only by boat. Travel from Hatteras Island to Nags Head, Roanoke Island, and the other northern parts of the Banks was also by boat. When NC 12 was completed, ferries would be important links, unifying the parts of the Outer Banks and their fragmented highway.

Ferry travel was not provided by the state of North Carolina in the early years, and privately operated ferry service formed the main connection between the mainland and the Outer Banks as well as between the separate parts of the Banks, especially Hatteras Island and Ocracoke Island. Private boat owners ran their craft between the mainland and the village of Ocracoke on the southern tip of Ocracoke Island for a few years, but in 1960 the state took over and bought the vessel *Sea Level* from the Taylor family, who had previously used that boat to run the route from the small seaport town of Atlantic to Ocracoke. Starting in May 1961, the state operated the *Sea Level* once a day between the two ports and charged a toll for passengers and automobiles. It was the first toll ferry operated by the state in North Carolina. Three years later, the state moved the docks from Atlantic to Cedar Island, which cut three miles off the journey. The reduction in distance, while small, meant the ferry could make two trips a day instead of just one, helping with the increasing number

Washington F. Baum in 1961, more than thirty years after he was responsible for building the Roanoke Sound Bridge, which was renamed for him
in honor of his efforts to connect the remote Outer Banks with the rest
of the world. (Courtesy of the Outer Banks History Center, Washington
Baum Papers)

of people seeking to cross the sound and inlet to reach Ocracoke. Once a highway was completed on Ocracoke Island, the number of visitors to the isle increased significantly, and in 1962 growing tourism forced the state to buy two new boats, the *Silver Lake* and the *Pamlico*. Starting that year, three boats would run the Ocracoke–Cedar Island transit.

A paved road had been built to reach Cedar Island from US 70 at Atlantic a few years before, making it easy for travelers to reach the new dock, and by 1966 this detour was shortened by three miles when a bypass cut Atlantic out of the loop altogether. The abbreviated trip from US 70 to Cedar Island ran along the twelve-mile-long paved road that the state labeled as State Road 1387. The short road would eventually become a part of NC 12, and the toll ferry route filled the breach between it and NC 12 on Ocracoke Island.

Before a paved road existed on Ocracoke Island, travelers who wanted to continue northward to Hatteras Island, or even farther, could ride a local bus along the length of the island to reach Hatteras Inlet. From there, they could catch a ferry on to Hatteras Island. Private operators ran the ferry service there, too. For three decades, starting before 1930, fishermen and other private boat owners carried passengers and an occasional automobile across the two-mile-wide Hatteras inlet, charging a dollar per person and two dollars per car. Frazier Peele was the last operator to run the ferry service there, using a boat that could carry up to four automobiles. The state bought out his operation and his boat in 1957 and began a toll-free ferry service that continues today, although much larger boats are used now.

Traffic across Ocracoke Inlet and Hatteras Inlet grew heavier through the years, but it was nothing like that between Hatteras Island and the Nags Head and Roanoke Island areas. The second inlet formed by the great storm of 1846 divided those areas, and it was a substantial break, not so much in size as in importance. When the hurricane struck and the wind and waves tore the channel through that central section of the Outer Banks, a freighter was coasting just offshore from Nags Head. The storm caught this ship and forced it through the new opening. Some say that the crew guided the craft through the break, but regardless of how it happened, after the storm subsided, the vessel was out of the Atlantic Ocean and drifting in Pamlico Sound. The ship, the *Oregon*, was the first ship to pass through the newly formed inlet, and henceforth the channel was called Oregon Inlet. The location of the inlet created serious problems since it blocked movement between Hatteras Island and the commercial districts around Nags Head as well as to Manteo, where trade was active.

After Oregon Inlet formed, it gradually widened and migrated southward, increasing the barrier that it represented for travel between Hatteras Island and the northern Banks. Although the inlet was a boon to fishermen, who could now take their boats between the sound and the ocean, it was about two miles wide and a hindrance to travel up and down the Banks, especially if one were riding in an automobile.

Even before roads were paved on the Outer Banks or bridges were built to reach there, the crossing of Oregon Inlet was a significant problem for both locals and visitors. Those wanting to travel across the break for either business or pleasure had few options until a local fisherman, Captain Jack Nelson, came up with a temporary solution in 1924. Nelson lived on Colington Island, a small offshoot of the Banks just west of Kill Devil Hills, and he started towing a small barge behind his fishing boat to transport paying customers across the inlet, initiating the first rudimentary ferry travel at the locale. He abandoned the project after only a few months, but it was taken over by Toby Tillett, another local boat owner who lived on nearby Roanoke Island. Employing ever-larger tugs and barges, Captain Tillett struggled to adapt his ferry service to the steadily increasing number of travelers crossing the inlet over the next quarter century. During all those years, his small-time operation was the only ferry service at the critical junction.

Starting in 1934, although the state had neither instituted

Before the days of concrete spans, bridges to the Outer Banks were built of wood, steel, and hard labor. (Courtesy of the Outer Banks History Center, Ben Dixon MacNeill Collection)

a ferry department nor offered any ferry service, North Carolina began subsidizing Tillett's operations to lower the costs for passengers and their cars. Tillett was still in charge, but state support made the tolls as little as ten cents for a passenger and fifty cents for an automobile. Yet the Outer Banks were experiencing hard economic times due to the Depression, and so even the lower prices were a hardship for many. In 1942 the State Highway Commission began to pay all costs for the ferry ride across Oregon Inlet, making it free for all riders a well as their cars. When the commission established the North Carolina Ferry Division in 1947, they allowed Tillett to continue his private ferry service until 1950, when they bought him out. The state purchased four converted navy landing craft and turned them into ferryboats to help with the increasing burden of passengers and vehicles crossing Oregon Inlet. The ferries, the *Herbert C. Bonner, Governor Umstead, Lindsey Warren,* and *Conrad Wirth*, ran every thirty minutes each way and ran all day during the summer when traffic was heaviest. After the state took over the ferry operations, within five years almost 100,000 vehicles and more than double that number of passengers were being transported across Oregon Inlet annually.

Traffic across Oregon Inlet continued to grow by leaps and bounds, and in 1956 acting governor Luther Hodges designated half a million dollars for new ferries that could handle larger loads and do so with greater efficiency in the years that followed. The new boats were designed to carry twenty-four cars instead of just eighteen, the maximum for the older ferries, and up to 120 passengers. They also had diesel engines that gave them speeds of twelve knots rather than the seven knots of the earlier craft. The new vessels increased the effectiveness of the ferry service, transporting travelers at almost double the rate of the older system. The new ferries had propellers at both ends, allowing them to be docked from either direction and eliminating the need to back into the landing area.

Named the *Sandy Graham, Emmet Winslow,* and *Governor Cherry*, the boats entered service in the summer of 1957, but they were still unable to meet the increasing demands of travelers wanting to cross Oregon Inlet and drive along the Outer Banks. Designation of most of Hatteras Island as part of the Cape Hatteras National Seashore in 1953 caused a leap in the number of visitors to the island, putting increasing pressure on the state system. Heavy traffic at Oregon Inlet caused long lines of cars to form, and waiting times were extensive. Discussion began about the possibility of building a bridge across the inlet and eliminating the ferries entirely.

The number of travelers crossing Oregon Inlet annually reached almost a quarter million by 1956, and the National Park Service expected this number to increase tenfold over the next ten years. Instead of three or four ferries, thirty or

Rare ice floes caused damage to the new bridges to the Outer Banks in the early twentieth century. (Courtesy of the Outer Banks History Center, Ben Dixon MacNeill Collection)

forty might be needed a decade later. The Oregon Inlet ferry situation had become so serious by 1960 that the state determined a bridge must be placed over the inlet at the earliest possible time.

Planning for the needed structure got under way in 1961. The proposed $4 million bridge would stretch two and a half miles across the tumultuous and dangerous waters of Oregon Inlet and connect Bodie Island with Pea Island. The federal government would provide half the money, but North Carolina would still have had to come up with $2 million had not First District representative Herbert C. Bonner managed to get legislation passed in Congress that reduced the state's share to just $1.5 million. That amount was still a substantial expenditure, but expenses for running the ferry service over the inlet had reached $500,000 annually. The elimination of that cost would allow the bridge to pay for itself in just eight years and North Carolina's outlay in only three.

The decision to build the bridge was a momentous event for locals and visitors alike and an unexpected blessing for residents of Hatteras Island. Bids were let in January, 1962, and construction started just three months later. The design for the high, curving overpass provided a roadway twenty-eight feet wide for cars and offered sixty-five feet of clearance through a distance of 180 feet for boats to travel underneath. The bridge was meant to withstand winds of up to 120 miles per hour and had no draw section because of its height. Electric transmission lines serving the entire population of Hatteras Island were carried by the structure, giving it a dual purpose. McLean Construction Company of Baltimore, Maryland, built the bridge and finished seven months early, thereby saving another $300,000 in ferry costs.

The Oregon Inlet bridge was dedicated on November 12, 1963, and opened to traffic eight days later. There was a proposal to name the new span after Toby Tillett, who operated the ferry service over the inlet for decades, and many on the Outer Banks agreed with that suggestion. However, Congressman Bonner had saved the state half a million dollars of the construction costs, and it was decided to name the bridge for him instead. Tillett had died a few years earlier, and although his family members were invited to participate in the dedication ceremony, none came.

The Herbert C. Bonner Bridge opened Hatteras Island to visitation and commerce in ways that even residents of the island could not not anticipated. It linked the road from Whalebone Junction with the road on Pea Island, and Hatteras locals who had once protested bitterly against the bridge's construction, and had even fought the building of a road there, stated now that it was the best thing that had ever happened to the formerly isolated island. Business on Hatteras Island boomed, and the convenience of access, with its resultant effects on the economy, was something that was beyond their wildest dreams.

The bridge was also intended to help fishermen. Twelve-hundred-foot-long fishing walks were constructed on both sides at the end to accommodate the many sportsmen who craved fishing in the prolific waters of Oregon Inlet. Fishing had been tried from the earlier bridges at Roanoke and Currituck Sounds, but the narrow passageway for cars left little room for anyone trying to drop a hook and line over the side rails.

The Herbert C. Bonner Bridge had graceful, curving lines and provided a high vantage point for viewing the beautiful churning waters of the inlet. Maintenance costs also made it the most expensive bridge in the state for the Highway Commission to support. Oregon Inlet itself, in constant turmoil from shifting currents and migrating shoals, saw steady erosion of the southern shores, including those parts under the support beams of the bridge. Concrete forms and metal supports were worn away or rusted continually by the force of the tides and from the salty air. Patching the concrete and replenishing the sand on the eroding shoreline were a constant demand, especially after storms.

Dredging the inlet was also an ongoing struggle. Shifting sand filled the inlet, making it difficult for boats to pass safely through the waterway without harming the bridge. Like other places on the Outer Banks, parts of the area around the inlet eroded while other parts accreted, causing a shift of the channel to the south as it gradually ate away at Pea Island. Erosion and weather threatened the Herbert C. Bonner Bridge and its critical function, just as those elements threatened the Outer Banks themselves.

Despite the hazards the new bridge faced, it filled an extremely important niche in the concept of the building of the Beach Road and filled a critical gap in the vital highway itself. The concrete-and-steel span was well constructed and designed to last for a quarter century, during which time the bridge would save millions of dollars in ferry costs and improve passage for visitors and locals as well. Because Oregon Inlet sits astride almost the midpoint of the Outer Banks, it created a serious hurdle for drivers, but the Herbert C. Bonner Bridge changed all that.

Just as the Washington Baum Bridge and the Wright Memorial Bridge stimulated commercial success for the northern Banks, the Herbert C. Bonner Bridge created similar effects for Hatteras and Ocracoke Islands. The unbounded construction and development seen from Kitty Hawk to Whalebone Junction would not be found on Hatteras Island or Ocracoke Island, however, because the major portions of those two isles were protected as part of the Cape Hatteras National Seashore. But business there began to grow.

But more than business was affected, for the new bridge ended the partition that had thwarted travel and development since Oregon Inlet was sliced through the Banks more than a hundred years earlier, and now the sheltered islands of Hatteras and Ocracoke were opened to continual and substantial visitation. The existence of the bridge represented much more than just a small, new part of the Outer Banks highway; it was symbolic of the elimination of the significant schism that had kept the parts of the Banks separate and disengaged from each other for so long. The Herbert C. Bonner Bridge signified the end of one era and the start of another.

For the first time, one could drive on a well-maintained, paved road all the way from a little north of the community of Duck to the village of Ocracoke on the southern tip of the Banks. Granted, that highway was a composite of small sections of roadway with different ages, diverse ancestry, and discrete labels, as well as a major bridge and one short ferry ride, but they were all joined end to end. State officials saw that connection and recognized the kinship within the collage of all the bits and pieces of paved road that stretched for so long along the formerly isolated barrier-island chain. In 1963 they chose to merge all the separate pieces of road, eliminate their individual names, and form a single major roadway that would become the future Outer Banks highway. They called that ribbon of pavement North Carolina Highway 12.

Additions were made to the new road during the next

twenty-five years. State Road 1387, the dozen miles of road between US 70 and the ferry docks at Cedar Island, officially became a part of NC 12 in 1975. An additional five miles of pavement, which had been gated and only available to land-owners of a new development built by private enterprise north of Duck in the late seventies, was taken over by the state in 1984. North Carolina removed the gates and made that short piece of highway part of NC 12. Finally, in 1985 the state paved passage from the end of the former private road all the way through Corolla to the edge of the beach just a half mile north of the small village. In 1987 that segment of road was named as part of NC 12, too, and it was the final link of asphalt that joined the barrier-island chain from one end to the other. NC 12 was complete at last and ran the entire length of the Outer Banks from the edge of the surging waves north of Corolla to the lapping ripples of Pamlico Sound at the southern tip of Ocracoke Island, and beyond there to the mainland, where it led through the picturesque setting of Cedar Island.

NC 12 stretches across four counties, 123 miles of sand, and another 29 miles of water to provide a route to all the parks, refuges, towns, history, and adventures offered by this formerly remote region where few wanted to dwell and even fewer chose to visit. One road changed all that. The Bonner Bridge, the ferries across Hatteras Inlet, and those that run between Ocracoke and the mainland are major contributors to traveling along NC 12; they provide its missing links so that one can truly make the journey to the distant site as well as navigate the Outer Banks from end to end.

North Carolina once had a highway called NC 12, but the name was changed many years ago, and the Outer Banks road is now the only one to bear that title. Perhaps it is fit-ting that such a distinctive highway should have a name all its own. And while the road is narrow and too short for some to consider it a major highway, NC 12 carries millions of visi-tors every year to the scenic and historic sites with which the Outer Banks are blessed. The slim strip of pavement also stirs controversy and debate. The Outer Banks finally got their Beach Road after years of intermittent and sporadic progress, and although the highway opened a new epoch in the development and appeal of North Carolina's barrier-island chain, whether it will remain there despite all the storms of nature and of human protest is now the major question. That query has no easy answers.

DISRUPTION AND CONTINUITY

As important as NC 12 was for the Outer Banks and their residents, visitors, and commerce, not everyone saw the road as an asset. Geologists were sure the Banks had survived the ages by natural processes where water and sand flowed unencumbered about the barrier islands, and some advocates were convinced that trying to maintain a roadway along the Banks would interfere with the flow of water and sand, and that keeping the road intact would require movement of vast amounts of sand, changing the nature of the beach and of the dunes as well. They assumed this could only put the Outer Banks at greater risk.

In the thirties, even before roads were built across the Outer Banks, man-made structures were installed that changed the landscape and perhaps natural forces on the Banks too. The Civilian Conservation Corps (CCC) and the Works Progress Administration (WPA) employed workers to protect the Outer Banks from erosion by building miles of dunes along the beaches to thwart the waves, which were wont to wash across the narrow ribbon of sand. They also planted sea oats and cord grass to cover the new dune line, built miles of wind fences, and set out thousands of trees and shrubs. The intention was to fend off the waves and the effects of storms to keep the Banks from being destroyed or eroding away, as well as to protect the cottages and businesses that had been built there. But some thought this strategy did more harm than good because the artificial arrangements could disrupt the

When ice floes smashed against the Wright Memorial Bridge, it was left too broken for passage, temporarily cutting off access to the Banks by that route. (Courtesy of the Outer Banks History Center, Ben Dixon Mac-Neill Collection)

usual transfer of sand that sustained the Banks and actually might cause them to deteriorate sooner.

Property owners on the Outer Banks were just as convinced that without the dune line and other protective measures of the CCC and the WPA, they were at the mercy of every storm, of which there were many. The row of artificial sand hills has, in fact, kept the ocean from destroying many of the homes that were built along the exposed edges of the Banks, and it has protected the narrow NC 12 as well. To accomplish this, the dune barrier has been rebuilt and the sand replenished many times through the years, at considerable expense and despite much heated discussion.

There is little doubt that artificial dunes keep normal waves from washing away the sand and the man-made structures that lie behind them, but dunes actually change the angle at which the waves strike, giving them a more devastating punch, and the waves generated by hurricanes or nor'easters are not to be considered normal. Hatteras Island has numerous sections where the strip of land is thin and the ground level low, making it vulnerable to powerful storms. Wind-driven waves have the strength to tear across the islands, wiping out cottages and parts of NC 12. Powerful, storm-fed waves have recently washed inlets through the exposed ground that lies between Oregon Inlet and Rodanthe on Hatteras Island, as well as at other fragile places.

More than a dozen different inlet sites have appeared on maps of the Outer Banks through the years, showing that their coming and going is nothing new, so it is highly likely that more inlets will be formed there in the future. Whether construction on the Banks by humans has increased the pace of inlet formation is still to be determined, but there is little doubt that the effects of inlet formation are increasingly serious for commercial development there and costly for all concerned. Trying to maintain a road on the Banks is just one aspect of this cost and development, but it is a key component.

"New Inlet," located just north of Rodanthe on Hatteras Island, is a rift that has come and gone numerous times through the centuries. The gap is known to have existed in this region as early as 1733 but later became clogged with sand. The inlet showed up again on maps in 1798 but could not be found in 1922. In 1924 the former inlet was dredged open to benefit fishermen who used the passage as an avenue to get through the Banks from the sounds to the ocean, but within a year the opening had shoaled up again. The inlet reopened on its own in 1932 and continued to open and close intermittently over the next decade. A storm tore the furrow open again in 1944, but only for a brief period, and after it closed the inlet did not open again for decades. When a hurricane reopened the channel in the twenty-first century, it was ironically called "New Inlet" again, despite the fact that there was nothing new about the feature. The only thing novel was that the breach washed out a goodly part of NC 12.

Some believe that NC 12 itself poses a risk to the longevity of the Outer Banks because the highway and its maintenance interfere with the natural processes that have nourished and restored the barrier-island chain throughout its existence. Others see the road as more of a victim than a culprit, and there is little doubt that NC 12 has suffered frequently from the assaults rendered by hurricanes and nor'easters. Whether the highway has aided and abetted the destruction caused by these storms, or has led to increased deterioration due to erosion or the blocking of natural restoration, is still debated without firm conclusions.

Atlantic storms and NC 12 are eternal antagonists, and NC 12 usually comes out the loser in any battles. Nor'easters and hurricanes have pounded the Outer Banks for centuries, some so severely that they are entrenched in the memories of those who live there as well as those who learn about them. Nor'easters, unlike hurricanes, sometimes sit in place for days before moving away, and this longevity can make them more damaging despite the fact that hurricane winds are usually stronger. Both types of storms threaten those who live on or visit the Outer Banks and also menace the little thread of pavement that connects the various parts of the land formation.

The Ash Wednesday Storm

The great storm that hit the Outer Banks in March 1962 was one of the nastiest nor'easters in modern memory. Listed by the U.S. Weather Service as one of the ten worst U.S. storms of the last century, the gale lasted for four days—three of which were spent lingering over the eastern coastline. The storm developed during a period when the alignment of the sun and moon caused unusually high tides along the North Carolina shores, magnifying the effects and the damage. The severe tempest sat atop the coastline through five cycles of high tides, and the elevated water levels added to the destruction. Wind strength surpassed seventy miles per hour, and the storm might have qualified as a hurricane had the season been right. The low-pressure storm generated waves more than thirty feet height, seriously damaging or destroying 2,000 homes on the Outer Banks.

The storm cut an inlet through Hatteras Island north of the village of Buxton, separating the small town from its neighbor Avon. It also sliced through NC 12, isolating the southern end of the island and stranding the folks who lived there. The inlet was a handicap to tourism and also stifled the movement of residents. Hatteras locals tried to remedy the problem by rounding up all the old junk cars and trucks they could find and dumping them into the channel. All such efforts were futile until dredges came in and moved sand into the breach, restoring the land to previous levels so the highway could be replaced.

While the loss of sand hampered the flow of traffic on lower Hatteras Island, the accumulation of sand obstructed NC 12 in the northern areas of the Banks. Erosion removed sand from the beaches around Nags Head, Kitty Hawk, and Kill Devil Hills, where wind and high water transported silt onto the road. Several feet of sand piled up atop the pavement and blocked normal travel through most of the region, so only four-wheel-drive vehicles were able to use NC 12. Wreckage from damaged beach cottages littered the roadway as well.

The 1962 nor'easter created major destruction throughout the Outer Banks, causing storm damage unlike any seen there in recent memory. The fiercest violence occurred on Ash Wednesday, so the tempest became known thereafter as the Ash Wednesday Storm, and few on the Outer Banks would ever forget it.

Fortunately, nor'easters of that intense level are not common, and those that do arise are phenomena of the winter and spring months, not the usual times for heavy tourism. Hurricanes, on the other hand, form off the coast of Africa and in the Caribbean every year and strike out in the general direction of the United States between June and December.

The completion of the Wright Memorial Bridge was accompanied by a proud archway near Kitty Hawk welcoming visitors to the "Birthplace of the Nation" and the "Birthplace of Aviation." Thousands came the very first year. (Courtesy of the Outer Banks History Center, Willard Jones Postcard Collection)

Their courses appear to be somewhat unpredictable, leaving forecasters in doubt about their eventual destinations, but they actually follow tracks determined by oceanic and atmospheric steering currents. Computer analyses can often forecast their targets with some certainty. Unfortunately, calculated landfall for hurricanes is usually accurate only within a couple of days, barely leaving time for necessary evacuation. On the Outer Banks, of course, that evacuation is for people only, not for the Banks themselves—and not for NC 12, which cannot leave, at least not voluntarily. The highway must bear whatever hazards nature produces when storms strike the barrier islands. Given the exposed position of the Banks, it is surprising that so few hurricanes rake the area with full force. Yet when they do hit, the damage can be enormous and devastating to the vulnerable region.

There is only a small chance a hurricane will strike North Carolina in any given year, but history has shown that almost one out of every five such storms formed in the Atlantic will affect the state to some degree. Some believe that, as the earth emerges from the last Ice Age, global climate change will influence the planet's weather trends, causing additional and more powerful storms to evolve. In the past thirty years, almost half again as many hurricanes have impacted North Carolina as in the previous three decades, adding credibility to such theories. Four major hurricanes, Isabel in 2003, Earl in 2009, Irene in 2011, and Sandy in 2012, have hit or brushed closely by the Outer Banks in the past dozen years. Earl brought high winds and erosion that affected NC 12 and damaged the areas between Rodanthe and Oregon Inlet, but by the time the hurricane arrived off the coast of North Carolina, it had diminished from a Category 4 to a Category 2 storm on the Saffir-Simpson Scale. The center of the storm also remained pretty far at sea, so other than causing beach erosion and creating several power outages, Earl caused little significant damage on the Banks. Isabel and Irene were potentially weaker storms but struck the Outer Banks more directly and with greater fury. Sandy was worse than any of these, but it did not hit the Banks with full potential.

Hurricane Isabel

Locals on the Outer Banks are no strangers to hurricanes, and names like Bertha, Fran, and Floyd stir painful memories of the destruction committed by those storms, including flooding, erosion, and the other damaging actions from wind, waves, and rainfall. But Isabel, barely a Category 2 storm, shocked everyone with the destruction it inflicted upon the Outer Banks. Early in Isabel's formation, weather forecasters rated the storm as a Category 4 since winds in excess of 165 miles per hour were produced near its center, but when the hurricane came ashore on September 18, 2003, the strongest gusts were only about 105 miles per hour. The Banks began to feel the onslaught more than twelve hours before the center made landfall, and the waves eventually grew to more than twenty feet high with a storm surge of almost ten feet. The actual height of the storm surge is uncertain since the gauge meant to measure it was demolished when Isabel struck.

Isabel damaged thousands of homes and businesses in Dare County, sweeping dozens of cottages and several motels off their foundations. The combined forces of wind and wave wrecked piers from Frisco to Nags Head, damaging them severely or destroying them completely. NC 12 was not impervious to this assault; the severe surf and rough waves created unusual destruction as parts of the highway were washed away or covered with sand and other storm debris. The worst mutilation occurred between Frisco and Hatteras, where waves and high water carved a major inlet. The island-spanning breach had three different channels and a total width of almost a half mile. The creation of the inlet caused that entire section of NC 12 to disappear.

Residents and tourists at the lower end of Hatteras Island who did not heed the warnings to evacuate were isolated by the large gap in the road, as well as by other washouts along

Even before NC 12 was finished, traffic to the Outer Banks was enough to require continual repairs to the Wright Memorial Bridge. (Courtesy of the Outer Banks History Center, Ben Dixon MacNeill Collection)

its route. Those who left before the storm were unable to return for weeks. The storm temporarily halted ferry service across Hatteras Inlet, and for the next few weeks, there was no place for the hundreds of stranded people on the southern end of the island to go. The rupture of the highway was so severe, and the inlet so deep, the North Carolina Department of Transportation (NCDOT) considered the possibility of building a bridge across the chasm or running a ferry service over the watery passageway rather than restoring the highway. In the end, the decision makers elected to refill the opening with sand and build NC 12 back over the restored ground. A massive amount of sand washed into Hatteras Inlet during the storm, and this source supplied the necessary fill dirt to close the storm-generated inlet, solving the problem of repairing NC 12. Elimination of the accumulated sand cleared the clogged inlet for renewed ferry travel as well.

Geologists were not happy with the decision to fill the breach and repave the road, for they realized that inlet formation was a critical phase of the Outer Banks's struggle to survive. They saw the presence of NC 12 as a problem and not a solution. But residents and visitors were happy because, more than two months after the storm, they were finally able to drive on NC 12 and were no longer isolated. Ferry service across Hatteras Inlet was also available again.

The storm proved to be an extremely costly episode in the battle by NCDOT to maintain NC 12, for the expenses ran to around $5 million, plus the additional expenditure of many hours of labor for their crews. But Isabel would not be the last hurricane to strike the Outer Banks and not the only one to wreak havoc on the tenuous highway.

Hurricane Irene

Eight years after Hurricane Isabel inflicted so much damage, another serious storm hit the Outer Banks with similar devastating effects—and some say worse. That storm was Hurricane Irene. Irene was not an especially powerful storm, but it was unusually large and slow moving, causing results that persisted much longer than from the average Atlantic hurricane. The gale came ashore on August 27, 2011, and moved up the Outer Banks by way of Pamlico Sound. High waves and rampaging surf washed away four significant portions of NC 12, three on Hatteras Island and one near Duck on the northern Banks. The worst breach was a 600-foot-wide opening just north of Rodanthe, but a 250-foot-wide opening was forced through NC 12 near Duck as well. On Hatteras Island, not only was the pavement eradicated but the underlying foundation of the road was stripped away as well, making repairs much more difficult and expensive.

The NCDOT was prepared for this particularly ruinous storm and quickly put plans into action to assist stranded residents and to restore NC 12 for travel. The Ferry Division set up temporary routes across Pamlico Sound from Stumpy Point, a small village on the mainland almost directly west of Oregon Inlet, to Rodanthe fifteen miles away, as well as to the town of Hatteras, which was about double that distance. The temporary provisional ferry service supported the isolated residents and also helped transport equipment for reconstruction. Ferries were a lifeline for severely damaged Hatteras Island, and after NC 12 was restored and travel returned to normal, the U.S. Coast Guard recognized the Ferry Division for Outstanding Humanitarian Response and presented its employees with a commendation for their work following Hurricane Irene's massive destruction.

At the point of the most severe disruption of NC 12 near Pea Island, NCDOT brought in a modular bridge that they assembled over the breach in fairly short order to reinstate travel along the NC 12 route between Oregon Inlet and Rodanthe. In just six weeks, engineers and crews emplaced the 650-foot-long span over the channel, where it rested upon more than eighty pilings and twelve concrete footings. Although NCDOT installed the bridge as a temporary measure, it was able to be used as long as necessary and remained in place until other corrections could be made in the roadway. Workers installed new pavement over the bridge and along its approaches all the way to Rodanthe. By October 10, 2011, almost two months after Irene hit, NC 12 was reopened for regular travel.

After the experience with Irene, the NCDOT began work with engineering experts as well as environmental, local, state, and federal officials to prepare a long-term plan for the maintenance of NC 12. New designs were incorporated to keep the lifeline of the Outer Banks open or restored to service rapidly in case of future damage. One of the new systems to help in assessing damage and predicting the best way to make repairs when NC 12 is washed out or breached is called photogrammetry, a method that uses photographs from high-flying planes to assess damage to beaches and to NC 12. It helps in determining the exact depth of sand that has been removed by a storm and assists in judgments regarding the best remedies for making repairs. The supplemental use of emergency ferry travel to the mainland, bridging washouts, and even raising the road above the sand are also part of the new plans. Few doubted that the new procedures would be needed.

Just one year after Irene came the most dangerous storm yet. It was called Hurricane Sandy—and no doubt given more-derogatory names by those who were forced to endure that super storm's wrath in the autumn of 2012. It was lucky that the Outer Banks were only grazed by the edge of the calamitous super storm, which ricocheted off the barrier islands, saving its major impact for the northern tier of states from Virginia to New York. The side effects, though, were shocking to the Outer Banks and raised fears of the portent of other super storms that might pass here in years to come. When NC 12 was hit by this unusual Atlantic storm, the NCDOT was called on once again to rescue the highway and its human dependents by all means possible. The battles were getting more difficult, but North Carolina was getting wiser about handling the assaults by both hurricanes and nor'easters.

The Herbert C. Bonner Bridge

The bridge over Oregon Inlet is a major part of the NC 12 route and must endure the passage of storms too. Despite its age and the passage of years and considerable traffic, it has stood up well to all attacks. When Hurricane Irene hit Pea Island, the only significant effect on the bridge was that the storm stalled some needed repairs scheduled for September 2011 involving some three-quarters of a million dollars in repainting and replacement of steel girders, but the renovations were simply rescheduled for the spring of 2012, when the weather was calmer.

After crossing the new bridges, rutted sand was the usual way for cars to travel before paved roads were placed on the Banks. It was treacherous driving, but some managed to succeed—eventually. (Courtesy of the Outer Banks History Center, D. Victor Meekins Collection)

The Bonner Bridge offers an example that not all damage to NC 12 and its various components comes from storms. The bridge exists under constant threats from weather and the movement of Oregon Inlet, and it also faces risks from normal deterioration as well as from the many millions of vehicles that drive across it every year. Boats passing underneath it also pose a continual menace as they try to run the gauntlet of migrating shoals while at the same time avoid striking the support beams that secure the bridge to the ground.

The Bonner Bridge began to settle in the early years of its existence as Oregon Inlet changed and deepened, causing the giant span to warp. The shifting of weight on its support beams induced stress that caused a large crack to form in the concrete structure on the fifth day of April in 1978. The damage stopped the flow of traffic for several days, and brief, intermittent one-way passage was allowed a little over one week after the crack was detected. Hatteras Island residents suddenly realized how important the bridge had become for them when food supplies and even the mail had to be delivered by special means. Three dozen employees worked eleven hours a day every day of the week until the bridge was reopened on the first day of May. The first major failure of the bridge had occurred just fifteen years after it opened, and the cost of restoration was $160,000.

Ten years later, in 1989, the Bonner Bridge grew more unstable from the ongoing battle against the forces of nature and constant usage, stirring discussion of the need to replace it. After serving so many travelers during its first quarter century, the aging structure was nearing the end of its lifespan, which indeed had been initially predicted to last only twenty-five years.

As if the elements were not enough of a challenge for the bridge, boats navigating the channels and shoals beneath it had to be steered carefully lest they run into the bridge supports, endangering the bridge, the vessels themselves, and any travelers who might happen to be overhead. A storm blew a loose barge against the supports in 1993, knocking out an entire 369-foot section of the bridge, halting the flow of traffic, and cutting off the 4,000 residents of Hatteras Island and temporarily stranding tourists there. The collision also broke the power transmission line that stretched beneath the bridge and left the island without power. The repair costs of that disaster were $33 million, including $5 million to replace the section and over $15 million to build a 3,200-foot rock groin to protect the bridge's southern abutment from further erosion.

If requests for replacing the bridge had not been overwhelming before, they were now. Hatteras Island residents, tourists, and NCDOT officials all suggested that a new bridge should be built at the earliest possible time. On a rating of safety where 100 indicated the most safe, structural engineers gave the Herbert C. Bonner Bridge a score of 2. Locals claimed that they carried hammers in their automobiles for breaking out windows or simply rolled their windows down when crossing the bridge so they would not be trapped in their vehicles if the bridge collapsed. They also claimed warily that they could feel the whole span shaking when the wind blew, which was often.

Problems arose almost immediately over plans to construct a replacement for the graceful but deteriorating span. There was no question that the new bridge would start on Bodie Island, but there was plenty of uncertainty about where it should terminate. Not only was NC 12 subject to frequent washouts for a few miles southward of the current bridge, but most of the land between the Bonner Bridge and the town of Rodanthe, a little over twelve miles to the south, was part of the Pea Island National Wildlife Refuge. Wildlife officials and environmentalists immediately recognized the threat posed by placing the end of a new bridge on the northern end of Hatteras Island. The continual repair of NC 12 along that stretch likely would cost millions of dollars each year, and the maintenance would require the movement of large quantities of sand that might seriously disturb the nesting of birds and turtles there. They believed the bridge must bypass these areas and terminate at or beyond the town of Rodanthe.

Taking these worries into consideration, the NCDOT developed a series of different proposals for replacing the deteriorating bridge. Eventually, the number of suggestions was narrowed to just two: a short-bridge plan calling for a parallel bridge that would end up not far from its current Hatteras Island location, and a long-bridge plan requiring a bridge seventeen and a half miles long that would link Bodie Island with the area near Rodanthe.

The short-bridge plan would evolve in phases, with future adaptations required by storms and erosion of the dunes and

Commonly used ruts, like those between towns, were sometimes lined with boards to help drivers avoid getting stuck. (Courtesy of the Outer Banks History Center, D. Victor Meekins Collection)

NC 12. The scheme would include restoring and maintaining the highway in its present location by building dunes, hauling in sand, resurfacing lost pavement, and placing bridges at new washouts. The parallel plan might even include putting the highway on raised platforms at critical places.

In the long-bridge plan, a structure would be built far out into Pamlico Sound, circumventing the Pea Island Wildlife Refuge entirely. The new bridge would curve widely to the west around the northern tip of Hatteras Island, avoiding washouts from storms that could form inlets across the island and lead to NC 12 having to be rebuilt. The longer bridge would bypass all the bird nesting areas, leaving them safe from human interference, as had been intended by the establishment of the refuge.

At some of the worst areas for travel, where getting stuck was frequent, small bridges were sometimes constructed to offer some relief. (Courtesy of the Outer Banks History Center, D. Victor Meekins Collection)

Local residents and officials, leaders of the wildlife and environmental groups, directors of the NCDOT, National Park agents, and both state and federal government representatives held many meetings and consultations for discussion of the alternatives. Despite the many conferences and long hours of argument, advisement groups were unable to reach an accord, and the plans to replace the bridge languished in uncertainty for over twenty years. During that time, NCDOT spent millions of dollars trying to shore up the Bonner Bridge, dredging Oregon Inlet to allow boats to maneuver there without smashing into the bridge, attempting to manage the steady erosion that was eating at the base of the southern end of the bridge, and assuring residents and travelers that they could cross the bridge safely (albeit with hammers just in case).

In September 2003 the U.S. Fish and Wildlife Service suggested that placing the end of the replacement bridge inside the refuge would not be compatible with the National Wildlife Refuge System Improvement Act of 1997, and NCDOT signed a concurrence document that would eliminate the short-bridge alternative from consideration, leaving only the long-bridge plan for evaluation. But less than two months later, planning for the proposed Bonner Bridge replacement was put on a six-month hold until April 2003 to allow Dare County commissioners to develop an alternate plan of their own. The commissioners worried that the long-bridge plan would remove NC 12 from the area and, along with it, access to the Pea Island refuge. At that time, state transportation officials still believed the bridge would be completed by 2010.

Disagreements and quarrels continued about whether the state had any right to place the bridge on the northern tip of Hatteras Island and to maintain a road across the refuge, but it was discovered that when North Carolina donated the land for the refuge in 1951, conditions of the gift specified that ten acres on the end of the island and access to it would still belong to the state. Stipulations also provided for a permanent easement, assuring that a road could be placed across the refuge in the future. To finalize the establishment of the Pea Island refuge and to assure these conditions, Congress passed Public Law 229 that same year authorizing these rights in perpetuity. Therefore, the National Wildlife Refuge System Improvement Act of 1997 had no bearing on the legal rights of the state as they were assured by law 229. North Carolina officials realized now that they could not only place the bridge where they wanted but could put the road there, too, and maintain it as needed in the future.

Some still wanted to challenge the idea, but Assistant Secretary Craig Manson of the U.S. Department of the Interior supported the rights of the state, and the North Carolina Department of Transportation began to make plans to replace the bridge without further delay. No more considerations regarding the compatibility of the bridging plans with the Pea Island Wildlife Refuge were deemed necessary. Yet, in 2010, by which time officials had thought the bridge would be completed, numerous studies and discussions continued, including one titled "Final Environmental Impact Statement." Another environmental assessment revising that "Final" one was later reported by the NCDOT and the Federal Highway Administration declaring that no significant damage would be caused by the Parallel Bridge Corridor (short-bridge plan). The administration recommended pursuing that design and dropping the Pamlico Sound Bridge (long-bridge plan).

Many locals raised an outcry to have the bridge replaced immediately. They grew weary of the long years of debate with nothing being accomplished and the bridge continuing to get older, and perhaps even more dangerous. They complained that some who did not even live in the area were delaying progress with more interest in preserving birds and natural surroundings than in the safety and welfare of the people.

The parallel plan entailed uncertainties about what would be involved in maintaining traffic along NC 12 near the bridge, but those questions supposedly had become moot. One thing most people could agree on was that storms would continue to wash the sand and the road away from the low areas at the northern end of Hatteras Island. What they could not foresee was the cost of that erosion and how frequently problems might occur. The long bridge, on the other hand, could cost more than $1.5 billion just for initial construction expenses, many times greater than the projected costs of the parallel plan. Plus, access for visiting the bird refuge and viewing its creatures in their natural habitat, one of the reasons the refuge had been put there in the first place, would continue to be possible if NC 12 passed through the area.

NCDOT tried to move forward with their planning process, but lawsuits filed by the National Wildlife Federation and the Audubon Society continued to block progress, for

Hatteras Island sand had no sympathy for governors. Here, North Carolina governor J. Melville Broughton is forced to push his car after it became stuck. Later, Governor Cherry suffered a similar experience. The state soon paved a road there. (Courtesy of the Outer Banks History Center, D. Victor Meekins Collection)

those groups still saw the phased operations to maintain NC 12 as a possible threat to the wildlife in the refuge. As a result, North Carolina officials declared that the phased portion of the parallel plan would no longer be a consideration in which bridge plan to accept. By 2010 they selected the parallel bridge plan and dropped any plans to build a bridge that would reach far out into Pamlico Sound and cost well more than a billion dollars.

The U.S. Department of the Interior gave approval for the choice, and North Carolina's governor, Beverly Perdue, acted immediately to move the project forward once the Federal

Wise drivers trying to cross sandy areas of the Outer Banks tried to follow in the ruts of previous cars. It was still an uncertain venture. (Courtesy of the Outer Banks History Center, D. Victor Meekins Collection)

Highway Administration signed onto the plan. The NCDOT selected three teams to compete for the job, and bids were opened in June 2011. The struggle to replace the Bonner Bridge appeared to be finally over, although it turned out that was not yet true. The replacement of the bridge was an idea that Marc Basnight, former leader of the North Carolina Senate and Dare County representative, had been pushing for years. He understood the importance of the bridge to the Outer Banks, to the economy, to the residents there, and to tourism, but the controversy was not over, and though the wheels were in motion, legal action by environmental and wildlife groups would yet stall the proceedings.

In 2011 the Southern Environmental Law Center in Chapel

Hill, representing Defenders of Wildlife and the National Wildlife Refuge Association, initiated lawsuits on both state and federal levels to block the rebuilding of the Bonner Bridge. Those lawsuits successfully held up progress on replacement of the bridge for four years, until finally, in February 2015, a federal court mediator was appointed to settle the conflict. Both the Southern Environmental Law Center and the NCDOT filed jointly for the mediation and were willing to seek an acceptable plan that would meet the needs of both parties. The result was a compromise that both sides could accept, and in June 2015 the two groups settled their arguments, giving NCDOT the right to go ahead with the replacement of the failing bridge. To protect the area of northern Hatteras Island where the wildlife groups had greatest concerns, the idea for a bridge in Pamlico Sound that skirted the refuge while extending about seven miles parallel to Pea Island replaced the NCDOT plan to place raised roadways on the island itself. The new Bonner Bridge was expected to cost more than $200 million. Fifty years after the bridge over Oregon Inlet was first built, its replacement now had a price tag fifty times the cost of the original structure. The first bridge had been designed to last for around twenty-five years and had survived for twice its expected lifespan. The estimated cost of replacement had more than doubled during the two decades of delays, but the new arrangements for the two bridges would still cost much less than the originally proposed Pamlico Sound structure that would have stretched for more than seventeen miles to bypass Pea Island. It was an economical as well as cooperative decision by both the Southern Environmental Law Center and the NCDOT.

Environmentalists, wildlife advocates, and NCDOT officials were all pleased. It was not as if the NCDOT cared nothing about the wild creatures of the Outer Banks and their habitat. The plans to build a replacement for the Oregon Inlet bridge incorporated considerable efforts to protect and sustain the lives and habits of the fauna in and around Pea Island National Wildlife Refuge. Guidelines required scheduling

Before NC 12 reached the Corolla post office, Jeeps with 4-wheel drive offered a good way to check the mail without getting stuck. (Courtesy of the Outer Banks History Center, Aycock Brown Collection)

work times around the nesting habits of piping plovers and sea turtles and avoiding the use of lights at night that might distract egg-laying turtles or disorient the hatchlings. Strict rules about the use of equipment were devised, so that operations would not harm any bird or animal. Road signs must be minimized and their shapes designed to prevent predator birds such as hawks or gulls from perching on them to attack other creatures. The new Bonner Bridge, with initial work scheduled for 2016, should meet the needs of humans, birds, and other animals. It is a part of NC 12 that is long overdue.

NC 12 is a necessity for traveling along the Outer Banks for those who live there and those who just visit. But some still view the little narrow passage as a hazard that threatens the very existence of the things visitors come to see, for even if the road does not disturb wildlife, the movement of sand required to sustain it could threaten the survival of the outlying strip of sand and thus the many creatures that live there. The new, hybrid bridging plan will assure that it does not menace the "hot spots" on northern Hatteras Island where the road is most vulnerable nor any regional wildlife.

Former North Carolina governor Beverly Perdue has stated that people who live on the Outer Banks pay taxes like everyone else and have the right to a road for their travel like other North Carolinians. Many of the visitors to the Outer Banks might not be North Carolina citizens, but they, too, could argue that they have the right to visit such a magnificent area. Without NC 12, this would not be possible. If the beauty is there but no one is there to see it, what is its value?

CHAPTER

6

GETTING THERE

Now that NC Highway 12 joins the far ends of the Outer Banks and passes through all the towns and historic places in between, local residents have access to all those places and to the mainland as well. Visitation by outsiders is available in ways that hardly could have been imagined just a few decades earlier. All that is left for tourists is to gain access to the famous Beach Road.

Four corridors allow more than 7 million visitors to reach NC 12 and the Outer Banks every year. Two gateways lead to the northern Banks and two to the southern tip. To reach the northern Banks, travelers can cross Currituck Sound on US Highway 158 over the Wright Memorial Bridge from Point Harbor, just south of Elizabeth City, to Kitty Hawk, or they can ride over Roanoke Sound on US Highway 64 via the Washington F. Baum Bridge from Roanoke Island to Whalebone Junction. To get to the southern end of the Banks at Ocracoke Island, riders can catch ferries from Cedar Island or Swan Quarter on the mainland and reach Ocracoke village after about a twenty-five-mile jaunt across Pamlico Sound.

Wright Memorial Bridge

The highway over the Wright Memorial Bridge from the mainland to Kitty Hawk was originally named NC 34 in 1935, but the label was changed to US 158. So today, one crosses the bridge on US 158, which once continued along the Outer Banks from Kitty Hawk to Whalebone Junction. That portion

Four-wheel drive vehicles provided one of the surest ways to maneuver on the Banks without getting stuck, even in areas of common travel where the sand was more firmly packed. (Courtesy of the Outer Banks History Center, Aycock Brown Collection)

of US 158 was renamed the Virginia Dare Trail and eventually became a part of NC 12. Before reaching the bridge, US 158 arrives from the small North Carolina town of Barco, just twenty-five miles to the north and about thirty minutes from NC 12. At Barco, US 158 intersects VA 168, a toll road from the Norfolk, Portsmouth, and Chesapeake areas of Virginia, making NC 12 less than a two-hour drive from Norfolk and a convenient route from Virginia and the rest of the northeastern United States to the Outer Banks. US 158 is such a popular passageway that, despite it being a multilane road, traffic jams can occur near the Banks during the summer season.

From Barco, US 158 stretches across the northern part of North Carolina toward the western part of the state to

Mocksville just east of US Interstate 77. From Mocksville to the Outer Banks, the highway passes near the towns of Winston-Salem, Reidsville, Roxboro, Roanoke Rapids, and Henderson and intersects north/south interstate expressways US 85 and US 95 along the way. The many access points to US 158 and the recent growth and appeal of the northern areas of the Outer Banks have made the Wright Memorial Bridge the most heavily traveled of the four gateways. Popularity of this route and the associated traffic congestion have led to plans for a possible new toll bridge across Currituck Sound that would connect US 158 on the mainland with NC 12 near Corolla. The bridge would be funded by public and private sources, as well as by tolls, but will still require an investment of millions of dollars from North Carolina. With a possible opening date of 2017, the toll bridge would provide a welcome shortcut and open a fifth entryway to the Outer Banks.

Washington F. Baum Bridge

The Washington F. Baum Bridge is another major entrance to the Outer Banks, ranking second in popularity and use. The bridge is located a little more than a dozen miles from the Wright Memorial Bridge but cannot easily be reached from US 158. To cross the Washington F. Baum Bridge to reach the rest of the Outer Banks from Roanoke Island, one must first get to Roanoke Island. US Highway 64, known as the "Road from Murphy to Manteo," joins the mainland with Roanoke Island and leads from one end of the elongated state of North Carolina to the other, connecting Murphy, the state's westernmost county seat high in the Blue Ridge Mountains, to Manteo, the easternmost county seat on the flat sands of the coast. A North Carolina map shows the distance between the two towns to be 543 miles, but the distance as the crow flies is only about 450 miles—still a long way, but most visitors to the Outer Banks will not have come all the way from Murphy.

From Murphy, US 64 passes near Hendersonville, Morganton, Statesville, Lexington, Asheboro, Cary, Raleigh, Rocky

Early drivers often chose to drive between the surf and the wrack line, where the sand was packed hard by the pounding waves that provided an avenue almost as good as pavement and wider than most roads. (Courtesy of the Outer Banks History Center, Aycock Brown Collection)

Here, a driver takes advantage of the low tide to ride the firm sand between the edge of the waves and the wreck of the *G.A. Kohler*. Perhaps he was more fortunate than the *Kohler*. (Courtesy of the Outer Banks History Center, D. Victor Meekins Collection)

Mount, Tarboro, and Williamston as it spans the state. It crosses north/south interstate highways US 85, US 95, and US 77 as well. A multilane highway for about a third of its length, the road enlarges to a divided highway for a hundred miles or so between Cary and Williamston but becomes only a two-lane road during the last fifty miles from Plymouth to Roanoke Island. The last few miles are through picturesque areas of marshes, swamps, and pocosins, where the area is lightly populated and reminiscent of scenes from bygone years as the road passes through Pettigrew State Park, Pocosin Lakes National Wildlife Refuge, Alligator River National Wildlife Refuge, and across the Alligator River on a two-mile-long drawbridge where once only ferry crossing was possible. There are plans to rebuild the last fifty-mile leg of US 64 into a modern, multilane highway, but it will still pass through the same scenic surroundings.

Until recently, travelers to the Outer Banks on US 64 were routed through the interesting town of Manteo before crossing the Washington F. Baum Bridge. However, in the summer of 2002, a new five-mile-long bridge opened, bypassing that village. The new span, the Virginia Dare Memorial Bridge, carries visitors over the broad expanse of Croatan Sound on US 64 bypass, a quicker, though perhaps less interesting, path to the outer parts of the Banks. It also offers a more direct and faster way off the barrier islands in the event of evacuation due to storms. After US 64 crosses the Washington F. Baum Bridge to the Outer Banks, it joins NC 12 at Whalebone Junction.

Cedar Island Ferry

A third way to get to the Outer Banks, and next in order of demand, is not across a bridge but aboard a ferryboat. Toll ferries carry cars and passengers, pedestrians, and cyclists from Cedar Island to Ocracoke village. Starting at 7:00 A.M., ferries run throughout the day in varying numbers depending on the season. The ride across Pamlico Sound lasts for a little over two hours. The ferries run six or more daily trips from May to October, with four in the midseason and three in the offseason. It is advisable to check the schedule and to make reservations to avoid having to wait in long lines to board the boats. The Ferry Division of the NCDOT publishes schedules for all its boats, and one can call 1-800-BY-FERRY or contact www.ncferry.org to get schedules and information or to make reservations.

To reach the Cedar Island ferry landing, one should drive eastward along US Highway 70 and take the cutoff onto NC 12 near the small town of Sea Level. From that intersection, it is only a dozen miles to the docks. US 70 runs parallel to US 40 from Asheville in the western area of North Carolina through Hickory, Newton, Winston-Salem, Statesville, Burlington, Greensboro, and Raleigh before it diverges and continues eastward by Smithfield, Goldsboro, Kinston, New Bern, and Morehead City. It intersects US Interstates 77, 85, and 95 along its route. At Morehead City, it meets NC 24 from Charlotte and Fayetteville, and at New Bern, it joins with NC 17 from Wilmington and the southern coastal towns. US Highway 70 is mostly a divided or multilane highway before reaching Morehead City, but it becomes a two-lane road in the last thirty miles or so before reaching NC 12. Easy access produces heavy traffic, so around 30,000 vehicles ride the ferry from Cedar Island to Ocracoke in a given year.

Swan Quarter Ferry

The last approach to the Outer Banks over the sounds is also aboard a toll ferry and lasts about two and a half hours. Boats depart the docks at Swan Quarter, a small town that adjoins the Swanquarter National Wildlife Refuge on the southern end of Hyde County, and travel southeastward about two dozen miles across Pamlico Sound to reach the village of Ocracoke. The Swan Quarter ferry is less busy than the Cedar Island ferry and only makes about half as many trips each day,

Captain Toby Tillet, with his ferry boat *Barcelona*, provided the only way to cross Oregon Inlet with an automobile during the years before North Carolina began its own ferry service. (Courtesy of the Outer Banks History Center, David Stick Collection)

but it is still recommended that riders check schedules in advance and make reservations to avoid long wait times.

Three highways lead to Swan Quarter. The best road is US 264 that branches off from US 64 east of Raleigh at Zebulon. Like US 64 and US 158, it is a multilane or divided highway through most of its course, and only the last fifty miles consist of just two lanes. A second highway, NC 45, branches off US 64 at Plymouth to head southward to Swan Quarter. Highway NC 94 leaves US 64 at Columbia, North Carolina, and travels about forty miles to the ferry docks. It, too, is a double-lane highway and a good route. US Highway 264 is the only road going to Swan Quarter that passes through any major cities, namely Wilson and Greenville. Interestingly, after leaving

When Hatteras Island finally got its paved road, Tillet's ferryboat offered access to Nags Head or Roanoke Island, but because it could only carry a few cars, many had to wait in line for the next load. (Courtesy of the Outer Banks History Center, David Stick Collection)

Swan Quarter, US 264 heads almost directly north to rejoin US 64 just two miles short of the Virginia Dare Memorial Bridge, making it the only route that gives tourists direct access to either the northern Banks at Whalebone Junction or the southern Banks at Ocracoke.

The ferries to Ocracoke are reminders of the olden days when the only way to get to and from the Outer Banks was by boat. Some people choose to use them because of that history. However, ferries today are nothing like the improvised fishing boats and towed barges of former years. Boats traveling these routes today are "Sound Class" ferries over 200 feet long and fifty feet wide and with a draft of six feet or so. They are stable platforms for transit over the sound, which, although not deep, sometimes has choppy waves. Each ferry can carry up to fifty vehicles and 300 passengers. The Swan Quarter and Cedar Island ferries, designated as "motor vessels," include the *MV Pamlico*, *MV Cedar Island*, *MV Carteret*, *MV Silver Lake*, and the newest editions, the *MV Sea Level* and *MV Swan Quarter*.

Travel by Air

Not all tourists to the Outer Banks arrive by private automobile. Many live too far away to drive there, and some come from overseas. Long-distance travelers usually fly to a nearby airport, rent a car, and drive the rest of the way. Several international airports lie within a short radius of NC 12, though the most convenient one is not in North Carolina but in Virginia. It only takes about two hours to drive to NC 12 from Norfolk International Airport or from Newport News–Williamsburg International Airport via VA 168 and US 158. It only takes six hours or less to drive to the Outer Banks from four large airports in North Carolina. The closest is Wilmington International Airport, which is only 150 miles from Cedar Island, but it is not the quickest route since the ride aboard the ferry lasts for two hours and that time must be added to the total trip. The fastest way from within the state is from Raleigh-Durham International Airport, which is only 200 miles or about four hours from Whalebone Junction on US 64. Greensboro International Airport is another hour to the west, and Charlotte International Airport is one hour farther.

No matter how one gets to the Outer Banks, arrival there leads to NC Highway 12, which offers access to the barrier-island chain from one end to the other. It is a road that endured many agonies during its birth, as well as delays and controversy that spread its construction across decades, although it is hardly more than a hundred miles long and not very wide. It is in a location that leaves it continually exposed to danger and destruction. Restoring and maintaining the road is almost as distressing as its original development, and its future is uncertain, since weather, climate change, and human concerns all are likely to impact its further existence. But it has changed the face of the Outer Banks and opened them to visitors from all over the world. Without that highway, few would know the Outer Banks for what they are, and we would all be the poorer for that.

CHAPTER

7

A DRIVE DOWN NC HIGHWAY 12

After more than half a century of struggle, the highway known as NC 12 is finally finished and runs about 100 miles over land as well as nearly thirty miles across water to connect scattered portions of the Outer Banks. It extends another dozen miles through sandy marshes to tie the last ferry landing on Cedar Island to a major highway at the small town of Sea Level. Some have called that road the spinal cord of the Outer Banks, for it is truly like the nerve center that controls all action on North Carolina's far-reaching barrier-island chain.

As NC Highway 12 was pushed all the way to Corolla in the late 1980s, reaching the last original town located on the northern Outer Banks, it brought changes there that were both good and bad. While opening up that section of the Banks and spurring tremendous growth, the highway has introduced traffic congestion that waxes and wanes depending upon the season. The new stretch of highway also forced the famous Corolla ponies to move nearer to the Virginia state line, for the heavy traffic endangered their existence. The once free-roaming mustangs were removed from Corolla, and today fences and cattle-guard gates prevent their return. One must travel off NC 12 to view the remaining 125 animals where barbed wire further limits their movement.

NC Highway 12 has different local names at various places along its route, and this last northern piece is called Ocean Trail. NC 12 ends just north of Corolla, where pavement and sand merge only yards from the Atlantic Ocean. Although the pavement extends no farther, Ocean Trail continues another

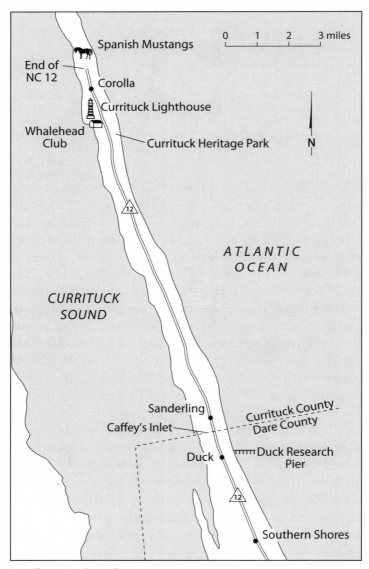

Corolla to Southern Shores

half mile across open beach to join Ocean Pearl Road, which connects with Sandfiddler Road to reach the Virginia border. These unpaved roads pass through three new housing developments called Swan Beach, North Swan Beach, and Carova, where safe driving is only possible aboard four-wheel-drive vehicles. NC 12 is unlikely to be paved beyond its current endpoint, for it would have to pass through protected parks and preserves. So, as in bygone years, where there is no NC 12, only sandy ruts await travelers.

A trip down NC Highway 12 from its northernmost tip to the ferry docks at Ocracoke will show a road with two quite divergent parts. From Corolla to Oregon Inlet, one finds crowded development and dense population, while from Oregon Inlet to Ocracoke, the environment is relatively unspoiled and the scattered towns have few permanent residents. These two sections of the Outer Banks have had very different histories, and the nature of the Banks themselves has caused the two branches of the road to evolve in disparate ways. The population of the northern Banks is five times that of the southern Banks, despite the smaller confines of the upper area, and even seasonal expansion is more pronounced north of Oregon Inlet.

Cruising the Northern Banks

The ride begins with NC 12 trailing to the south, passing through a close embrace of wind-twisted maritime growth as it approaches Corolla, just a half mile down the road. The pavement, already slender, seems even narrower as the scrubby growth pushes in from both sides and sand flung by the wind piles into drifting sheets onto its edges. If not blown away by the same wind that brought it, the sand must be removed by the North Carolina Department of Transportation. It is an ongoing battle, for sand and NC 12 coexist everywhere on the Outer Banks, sometimes as companions but often as adversaries. Storms only complicate the arrangement.

Before an asphalt highway crossed Hatteras Island, locals and visitors could travel between Oregon Inlet and the small villages on the island by riding the Manteo-Hatteras bus. Operated by the local Midgett family, the small buses traversed dunes and beaches for more than two decades with very few failures. (Courtesy of the Outer Banks History Center, Aycock Brown Collection)

Corolla appears suddenly, its structures bordering the road on both sides. Once a small, isolated village with no more than fifteen full-time residents, it is now a resort town with numerous residents and many vacationers. The spot was known as Jones Hill until 1895, when it acquired a post office and a new name—Corolla, a term referring to the petals of a flower. The northward extension of NC 12 from Duck to Corolla in the 1980s brought rapid, phenomenal growth as homes and businesses sprouted along the asphalt, making the former remote region almost unrecognizable. Today, the exclusive, costly cottages adjacent to the road are largely concealed by the surrounding maritime forest of gnarled oaks and twisted greenery, belying the real population of hundreds of permanent residents and thousands of temporary guests. Only the traffic jams that sometimes run from the Wright Memorial Bridge all the way to Corolla tell the true story.

The red-brick Currituck Lighthouse stands at Corolla within sight of the road, where it peeks over the trees to flash warnings across the sea it has guarded for so long. Other historic sites sit on Whalehead Bay in nearby Heritage Park just yards off the highway. These attractions and the beauty of the area bring multitudes of visitors each year, for NC 12 has opened the barely accessible region and turned it into a vacationer's paradise in just a quarter century.

Once past Corolla, the highway continues southward, skirting close to Currituck Sound since numerous cottages crowd the side near the beach. Deep shadows dapple the roadway as thickets of pines, stunted oaks, and other small trees partially shield it from the sun. The sprawling hedgerows, warped by the wind, help hide the many dwellings nestled there and conceal the waters of the sound and sea as well. Glimpses of Currituck Sound and the Atlantic Ocean occasionally steal through the façade, luring travelers off the main road and onto side streets for a closer look. Roads lead off both sides of NC 12, and some reach the sounds, but on the beach side, private roads that appear to lead to the beach often only provide access to the cottages. Local maps help show the public access areas to the beach and also indicate off-road parking. Signs located along NC 12 point the way as well.

Scenery changes little for the next four miles, as cottages, businesses, and scattered maritime growth line the highway. Biking and hiking trails from two to four feet wide are marked off on both sides of the pavement, but walking and pedaling along the busy road can be hazardous. Separate trails for pedestrians have been paved a short distance away from NC 12 at most places from Corolla to Kitty Hawk, alternating from one side to the other.

About five miles from its beginning, the highway passes

the Currituck Club golf development, which runs beside the road on the right for more than two miles, covering dunes, wetlands, flats, and maritime forest. Secluded cottages and scattered wooded areas continue to dominate the road on the beach side.

The Currituck Outer Banks Visitors Center is found on the right about a half mile past the golf resort and is worth a stop. It is a valuable source of information, offering maps and brochures, and also has restrooms. Just beyond there, NC 12 approaches Pine Island Audubon Sanctuary, which extends for four miles through the narrow confines between sound and road. Because it is a bird sanctuary, the number of buildings is limited, and the number of cottages on the beach side of the road also shrinks noticeably as the width of the Banks narrows to only about 200 yards. The proximity of the Atlantic Ocean and Currituck Sound gives one the eerie feeling that the sides of NC 12 are squeezing in even closer. The tight bottleneck is the former location of Caffey's Inlet, named for the farmer who owned the land before the inlet washed through in 1770. After the inlet closed in 1811, the site continued to bear the name, as did the Coast Guard station there. The inlet's closure cut off Currituck Sound from the Atlantic Ocean, changing the waters of the sound from salty or brackish to fresh. The change was welcomed by hunters and fishermen, since fresh water made the area more appealing to certain fish and to migratory birds. The location of the old inlet now forms the boundary between Currituck and Dare Counties. It also marks the change of the local name of NC 12 from Ocean Trail to Duck Road.

The land widens as Duck Road begins, and the number of cottages expands accordingly as NC 12 passes through the recently formed community of Sanderling. For the next five miles, beach cottages line the shore thickly, showing how Sanderling has grown into a popular area for both permanent and vacation homes. Most of the houses are on the beach side as Duck Road runs near the sound all the way to the

A young Stockton Midgett, who drove the Manteo-Hatteras bus when it was nearly lost in a sinkhole during a storm on Hatteras Island. (Courtesy of Tim Midgett)

next town, which, appropriately, is Duck. Just north of Duck, NC 12 passes what is said to be the greatest oceanic-research collection locale in the world, the Army Corps of Engineers Field Research Facility, where a pier equipped with advanced instruments and equipment reaches out over the Atlantic for a third of a mile.

Duck, the former secluded village that could only be reached by a perilous drive through twelve lonely miles of gritty sand from Kitty Hawk, now is one of the most popular vacation spots on NC 12. The community was populated by a few indigenous Outer Bankers, mostly fishermen, until NC 12 was extended from the end of the Virginia Dare Trail. When tourists became able to reach its exquisite open beaches, Duck grew significantly to become one of the most visited places on the Outer Banks.

Some say the town was named for the wild fowl that have always congregated there in such large numbers, and that seems likely. Although the place was so wild and empty, the military established a bombing range on its outskirts during World War II, leading some to claim facetiously that perhaps it was named for having to dodge wayward missiles. However, the post office was named "Duck" as far back as the nineteenth century, discounting such theories. Incorporated in 2002, Duck was ranked that same year as one of America's Top Ten Best Beaches. Today, Duck has about 500 full-time residents, but the population swells to nearly 25,000 during the summer—all the result of access by NC 12, which now struggles to accommodate the growth it created.

NC 12, or Duck Road, barely leaves the town of Duck before it enters another flourishing but recently developed community called Southern Shores. The highway changes its local name again as it enters town, switching to Ocean Boulevard. The town was laid off for development in 1947 and incorporated in 1979, many years before its neighbor Duck, although that town had been around much longer. Southern Shores occupies about four square miles along beach and sound and is permanent home to nearly 3,000 residents as well as many

Passengers wait to board the Manteo-Hatteras bus on Hatteras Island. (Courtesy of Tim Midgett)

vacationers. All these closely packed towns are fed by NC 12, and the wide, clean beaches lead many visitors there during the warmer months.

Ocean Boulevard continues southward as it leaves Southern Shores and passes the Duck Woods Country Club before reaching the Kitty Hawk Pier, the first of several piers that stretch into the ocean between there and Whalebone Junction. The road changes its local name from Ocean Boulevard to Virginia Dare Trail as it goes by the pier. Recalling that the original paved road on the Outer Banks was the Virginia Dare Trail, it almost feels as if one has traveled with the road all across the barrier islands and then come back home again.

The Virginia Dare Trail, first paved on the Outer Banks eighty years ago, is said to have been named by Frank Stick,

David Stick's father, and leads into the part of the Banks that was first the center of activity. The character of the road changes here as the tree- and scrub-covered environment prevalent along the previous route is exchanged for openness where cottages are visible on all sides as far as the eye can see. Maritime forest is no longer found along the highway, and very few trees or bushes border the road here or for many miles to come.

Mileposts placed along the side of NC 12 from the beginning of the Virginia Dare Trail southward help inform travelers of their exact location, so this is Milepost o. The milepost idea belonged to David Stick, who saw it as an easy way to help people locate places along NC 12. Many businesses there now advertise their location by using the mileposts. Begun in 1979, the signs are even more important today because of the congestion of so many businesses and houses that line the roadway all the way to Whalebone Junction. The milepost scheme has also begun to be extended to Hatteras Island, although with so many empty miles between villages there, it is less noticed and not as valuable to travelers.

NC Highway 12 now enters the area of the Outer Banks that was fashionable among tourists as far back as the early nineteenth century. Visitors came here by boat before the sounds were bridged and the highway paved, but now they can cross the Wright Memorial Bridge just a couple of miles away or the Washington F. Baum Bridge near Whalebone Junction. The Virginia Dare Trail connects the entrances from the two bridges, as it has done since the 1930s, and has a history as the most popular route on the Outer Banks. It is still quite esteemed today.

It is important to note that the US Highway 158 bypass, known locally as the Croatan Highway, is a paved highway that runs parallel to the Virginia Dare Trail throughout the older road's route. The roads travel side by side only a quarter of a mile apart for about sixteen miles. As close as they are, they are light years apart in their characteristics. Streets

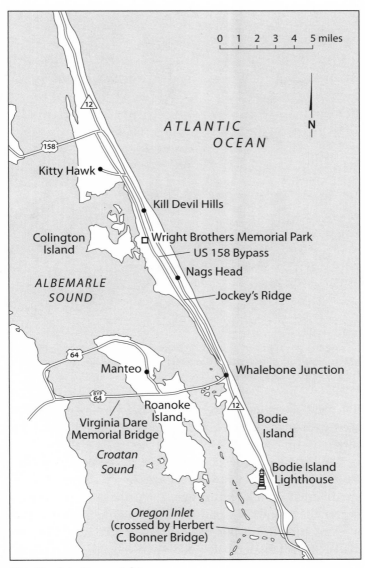

Kitty Hawk to Oregon Inlet

Fishing has always been popular on Hatteras Island, and driving on the beach was a part of that ritual. (Courtesy of the Outer Banks History Center, Aycock Brown Collection)

link them at frequent intervals, making movement between the two roadways easy, but that travel is much like passing through a time warp of a hundred years.

The Virginia Dare Trail runs close to the beach, passing among quiet, tranquil rows of cottages in scenes probably not too different from a century ago. The Croatan Highway runs nearer the sound; is a multilane thoroughfare filled with a modern complex of businesses, restaurants, and shopping malls; and is jammed with people and vehicles. The Croatan Highway, or US 158 bypass, is a place where the mileposts are really helpful.

NC Highway 12, or the Virginia Dare Trail, bears left as it heads southward from the intersection at Kitty Hawk, while US 158 bypass diverges to the right. The Aycock Brown Welcome Center, located directly across from the fork, not only aids travelers but represents a dividing point between the more-recent part of NC 12 and the original section where travelers visited the Outer Banks before there even was a highway. The welcome center is named for Aycock Brown, a local photographer who was interested not only in maintaining a pictorial record of the Outer Banks but also in publicizing the area widely to help it become the kind of tourist haven he believed it deserved to be. Hundreds of his photographs are located at the Outer Banks History Center in Manteo, where they, along with other exhibits at the center, are well worth a look.

After passing the intersection with US 158 bypass, NC 12 enters Kitty Hawk, one of the oldest towns on the Outer Banks. The village has been occupied for more than 200 years and was called Chickahauk as long ago as the 1700s. It is a title thought to be a Native American word meaning "The place of goose hunting." The word was probably mispronounced through the years by settlers who did not speak the language, and it gradually evolved into its modern form. It is an appealing name, befitting a town that is equally engaging. Kitty Hawk is where the Wright Brothers came to begin their experiments in flight, although those flights actually took place a little farther south.

The Virginia Dare Trail goes through Kitty Hawk, passing rows of what appear to be older cottages on both sides of the road. Many are painted in soft, pastel colors, and almost all are adorned with second-story and even third-story balconies where residents can try to catch a glimpse of the nearby Atlantic Ocean. During storms, the ocean comes much closer and sand washes over NC 12, sometimes blocking passage until it can be cleared. The highway here has been somewhat disrupted by these intrusions, and strips of patching tar cover the pavement in intricate scrawls, keeping it intact and safe for travel.

The highway hardly enters Kitty Hawk before it leaves the village behind. At Milepost 2, NC 12 enters Kill Devil Hills.

Driving on the beach is still popular now, especially among fishermen, and hundreds drive along NC 12 to reach the best locations. Some restrictions apply to driving there today. (Courtesy of the Outer Banks History Center, Drew Wilson Collection)

The Banks narrow here, but they soon expand again to a mile in width, which is still quite limited. Kill Devil Hills, like many of the early villages on the Outer Banks, has an intriguing name. Some say the place was named for a kind of rum made in England and salvaged from a wrecked ship nearby; it was so strong, it could "Kill the Devil." Others claim the numerous high sandy dunes there were so hard to climb that the effort could "Kill the Devil." No one knows for sure, but regardless of the name's origin, Kill Devil Hills and the adjoining town of Kitty Hawk represent the location where humankind first broke the bonds of gravity when Wilbur and Orville Wright flew their kite-like plane there early in the twentieth century, forever marking the site as the home of the first powered flight.

Cottages and an occasional gift shop or restaurant occupy both sides of NC 12 throughout the drive across Kill Devil Hills, and there is hardly an empty space on either side of the road. But the picturesque atmosphere is still peaceful and

North Carolina established a ferry service of its own in the 1950s, but waiting for the ride was still a common practice. (Courtesy of the Outer Banks History Center, Aycock Brown Collection)

reminiscent of an earlier age. The road passes Avalon Pier near the southern edge of town, and at Milepost 8 it passes the Wright Brothers National Memorial Park, which is actually located next to the bypass.

Milepost 10 marks the entry into Nags Head, once the most populated and popular town on the Outer Banks, although it would likely face some challengers for that title today. Homes and businesses are so closely packed together here that, without the town-limit sign, it would be impossible to know that one was leaving one town and entering another. However, the nature of the homes seems to change, as the dwellings in Nags Head appear both larger and more extravagant. Some older, simpler cottages can still be found, although many have washed away during the years, and others have been demolished or replaced. Some have called the older homes the "Unpainted Aristocracy" in honor of their history and their architectural style, and the ones that survive are surrounded by bigger, more luxurious—and clearly more expensive—edifices. Some of the more-recent cottages are unpainted, too, since many are covered on all surfaces by cedar shingles. Earlier cottages had a unique style with one and a half stories, large dormers, and distinctive canted-roof structure; but more relevant to their survival, they had no plumbing or chimneys to hold them to the ground. When storms threatened in the early years, the houses could be moved between beach and sound by placing them on rollers. It was an ingenious technique that saved many structures. The homes today have both chimneys and indoor plumbing, making them immobile and at the mercy of the weather, but in all fairness to them, their construction was necessary because many of the older homes were, in fact, eliminated by storms.

Outer Banks towns have special names with various theories to explain them, and Nags Head is no different. Some have suggested that local Outer Bankers once hung a lantern around the neck of a horse and led it along the shores to fool ship crews into thinking it was another ship, causing them to try to follow it and wreck on the shores to be looted. The history of those who lived on the Outer Banks is primarily one of rescue, not wrecking, so it seems unlikely that they would have resorted to such dastardly methods. The small population in the early years was so sparse that Bankers probably would not have been able to keep up with the hundreds of ships that marooned there, much less try to get more. But a horse is known as a nag, and it is a good story, so who can say? A less-dramatic theory is that the town is named for a pub or perhaps a shoreline feature in England.

The ride on the Virginia Dare Trail ends shortly after Milepost 16, where the road joins US Highway 64 and US 158 bypass. At that intersection, called Whalebone Junction, NC 12 moves farther west and away from the beach to follow more closely along the sound waters. Those who want to continue to drive along the beach can follow South Old Oregon Inlet Road for another two miles before it rejoins NC 12.

The Whalebone Junction Welcome Center at Milepost 17 provides information for travelers going either north or south and is located just south of Jennette's Pier. Jennette's Pier is famous for its aquarium and its reputation for good fishing, and many travelers along NC 12 stop there. Whalebone Junction is not so much a town as it is the place where a service station once stood that used an actual whalebone skeleton to attract business. The service station burned many years ago, and the whale skeleton disappeared, too, but the name has lingered. Whalebone Junction not only represents the intersection of several Outer Banks roads but also marks the entry into Cape Hatteras National Seashore. From here across Hatteras and Ocracoke Islands, NC Highway 12 has also been designated as a National Scenic Byway. The junction is notable, whalebones or not.

After Whalebone Junction, the Virginia Dare Trail becomes Cape Hatteras National Park Road. The National Park Service was the first to pave most of the Beach Road along this track, and the title honors that effort. Cape Hatteras National Park Road crosses Bodie Island—once called Cow Island, though it no longer is an island at all—and passes the Bodie Island Lighthouse. The black-and-white-striped beacon has stood there for almost 150 years and has recently been opened for visitors to climb for the first time. Just a couple of miles past the lighthouse, the road approaches Oregon Inlet, the hurricane-formed breach separating Hatteras Island from Nags Head and Roanoke Island. The site is the location of the Oregon Inlet Fishing Center and a U.S. Coast Guard station. More important, perhaps, is the fact that the end of the road marks the entrance to the Herbert C. Bonner Bridge, which carries NC 12 across the chasm and on to Hatteras Island, making the roadway continuous from Corolla to Hatteras village.

Driving over the Bonner Bridge across Oregon Inlet represents the crossing of the great rift that has separated the two major parts of the Outer Banks for more than a century. The divide is not only a geographical separation but a significant cultural disconnection that has created two very dissimilar areas in terms of their nature and characteristics. Even before the days of the Cape Hatteras National Seashore, the separation kept the rapid expansion and commercial development of the northern Banks away from the isolated islands of Hatteras and Ocracoke.

The Ride on Hatteras Island

Once across the lengthy span of Bonner Bridge, NC 12 disembarks onto Hatteras Island, where the road offers a totally different vista from any seen so far on the northern Banks, just a couple of miles away. It is a place where the highway faces the greatest threats to its existence, as do the Outer Banks themselves, for Hatteras Island is very narrow and barely above sea level, and it juts far out into the stormy Atlantic. From here southward, all the way to the village of Ocracoke, the Outer Banks are more delicate and natural because development has been limited by National Seashore restrictions since the 1950s, leaving views of sea, sound, and the island much as they have always been on the Banks.

Just south of the bridge, NC 12 enters Pea Island National Wildlife Refuge, where few buildings mar the scenery and no tall trees grow. The trees and shrubs are stunted, wind warped, and too low to block either the view or the continual breezes and waves that sweep over the sands. The land is flat, except for man-made dunes between the highway and the Atlantic, leaving vision unobstructed for miles. The panorama is different from any seen before on NC 12, as the absence of cottages, businesses, and maritime forest exposes an environment of sand, scrub, marsh, and water in every direction to the horizon. The Cape Hatteras National Seashore and the Pea Island National Wildlife Refuge have helped protect not only the wildlife but the inviolability of Hatteras Island as well.

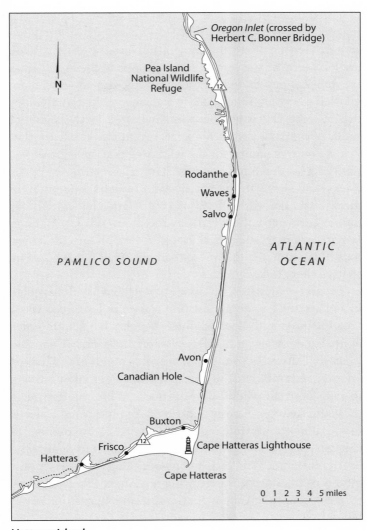

Hatteras Island

Three miles after NC 12 crosses the Bonner Bridge, the highway passes a small visitor center operated by the wildlife refuge. Viewing platforms for spotting birds or other wildlife are located near the center. Access ramps to the beach cross the dunes at designated locations nearby, and no vehicles are allowed to drive on the shore in the area, making it ideal for beachcombers. It is here, at this small oasis in the region of sand, salt marsh, and scrubby trees, that one can learn that Pea Island was named for the wild peas that once grew profusely across the dunes and flats. Those peas attracted geese, ducks, and swans to the nearby sound waters, making it an ideal winter home for migratory birds—and an ideal spot for hunters, who slew these birds by the thousands for shipping to northern markets, as well as to provide plumes for ladies' hats. It is estimated that more than 350 types of birds can be spotted there today.

To protect the birds, the area was declared a federal refuge in 1938, setting aside almost fifty square miles of protected area for birds and other wildlife—roughly ten square miles of land and forty square miles of water and marsh. Canoeing is possible throughout the marshes and sounds of the refuge, and marked trails starting at the visitor center allow viewers to enjoy both the wildlife and the flocks of birds. Some make the claim that there are as many types of biting bugs as birds in the refuge, and while a doubtful assertion, the number of chiggers, ticks, and mosquitoes is still sufficient to require the use of repellents. Wild peas still bloom along the dunes in soft muted colors during the growing season, so Pea Island remains appropriately named, even if it no longer is an island but only a part of Hatteras Island.

NC Highway 12 extends down a long straight path for a dozen miles through Pea Island before reaching the first small town, Rodanthe. A row of man-made dunes blocks views of the Atlantic along the route, but travelers are always aware of its proximity since the ocean follows closely by the highway and battering waves create a hazy mist that hangs in the air and sometimes drifts over the road. The flatness of

Although Hurricane Sandy struck the Outer Banks only a glancing blow, the water forced sand across NC 12 and washed out pavement, too, as vicious waves crashed across Hatteras Island. (Courtesy of North Carolina Department of Transportation Photogrammetry)

the sand, which in places barely rises above sea level, and the power of the Atlantic Ocean, which sits so close, leave little protection for NC 12 or for Hatteras Island either. When the tide is high and blustery winds blow from offshore, the combined effects can propel water and sand over the island and the road. Storms magnify that effect, and when hurricanes or nor'easters strike, damage to both NC 12 and Hatteras Island can be devastating.

The North Carolina Department of Transportation has designated some of the more-treacherous areas of the twelve

Artificial dunes constructed along the hot spots on Hatteras Island are intended to protect NC 12 from waves generated by storms, but those dunes often are annihilated, too, leaving the road exposed to the next storm. (Courtesy of North Carolina Department of Transportation Photogrammetry)

miles between the Bonner Bridge and Rodanthe as "hot spots" because of their special vulnerability. When one drives along the highway, there is incriminating evidence seen lying beside the road showing the aftereffects of wave action that confirms the NCDOT's analysis; inlets have been cut through Hatteras Island and across NC 12, where pavement has been cracked and tumbled into piles of debris. Although NCDOT is quick to mend the breaches and to repair the highway, the remnants of former destruction lie exposed along the road throughout the area, calling attention to the fragile nature of both the island and its road.

Numerous repairs to NC Highway 12 have made it a patch-work of old and new pavement all across Pea Island. Dark new pavement contrasts with older, grayer pavement from earlier applications, and discarded chunks of broken asphalt lie in heaps beside the road. A temporary bridge over 600 feet long has been placed across "New Inlet" about halfway down the refuge. The inlet is a recurring breach, but Hurricane Irene renewed it with a vengeance in 2011. The transitory bridge closed the storm-caused gap in NC 12 so traffic along Hatteras Island could be restored quickly. Though meant as a temporary link, it was intended to be replaced by a more-permanent structure nearly three miles long, for the inlet persists and tends to migrate. However, new plans to provide a bridge in Pamlico Sound to bypass the hot spot area have caused those plans to be discontinued. Dunes between the temporary bridge and the ocean protect the span, but sand is still washed or blown across it at times, requiring road machines to remove it, temporarily halting traffic.

All along NC 12 throughout the dozen miles of isolated hot spots, earth-moving equipment stands beside the road ready for clearing away sand washed or blown there. It is here, at these hot spots, that future plans for a bridge bypassing the treacherous zone are intended to protect NC 12 and help Hatteras Island survive as well. The movement of water and sand will be returned to its historic process, and the part of the region devoted to the preservation of birds should survive while access to see them is not hampered. It seemed a wise compromise between NCDOT and the environmentalists and wildlife organizations, and it will also permit the much-needed replacement of the Bonner Bridge.

As NC 12 approaches Rodanthe, it enters a zone known traditionally as the "S- Curves" just north of town. At one time, NC 12, which is notably straight along most of its path, had wavy curves at this point near Mirlo Beach, but this is one of the areas most susceptible to storm damage, and years of restoring the highway have gradually diminished the exaggerated curves. Some curvature is still found along this stretch

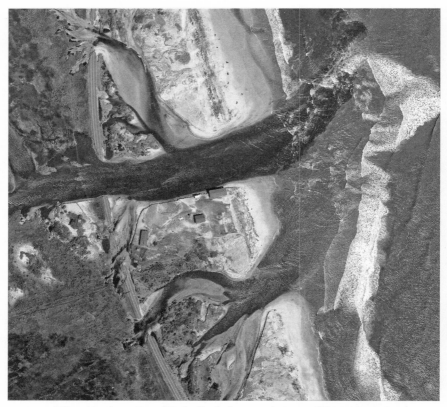

When Hurricane Irene hit the Banks in 2011, the powerful storm reopened the recurring breach across Hatteras Island known as "New Inlet." It washed away over a hundred yards of NC 12 in just that one place. (Courtesy of North Carolina Department of Transportation Photogrammetry)

of the highway, perhaps maintained by NCDOT in honor of the history. The "S-Curve" area remains a hot spot and suffers severe damage when hurricanes and nor'easters hit. When storms follow each other in close order, which is what happened with Isabel, Irene, and Sandy between 2003 and 2012, the devastation is not only harsh but also enduring, making the region more susceptible to damage from later, perhaps even milder, storms.

Mirlo Beach, an open area on Pamlico Sound popular for

its legendary surfboarding, sailboarding, and kiteboarding, is marked with piles of broken pavement that demonstrate the hazards of the hot spot. Across the road from Mirlo, giant sandbags form a barricade to hold the sea at bay. Loose sand is piled on top of the bags to form artificial dunes, which successfully protect the road except during severe storms.

The first cottages seen on the trip down Hatteras Island snuggle closely against the highway through Rodanthe, and just a half mile inside the town limits, on the left side of the highway, stands the Chicamacomico Life-Saving Station Historic Site and Museum, where the first of the original lifesaving stations stood on the Outer Banks. Chicamacomico is the only U.S. lifesaving station that still exists with its original buildings, which is a little surprising in such a storm-battered area. Built here on the easternmost projection of the Outer Banks, it was the closest place for spotting passing ships.

The station was first built in 1874 and continued to operate after the Lifesaving Service changed to the Coast Guard in 1915. It was here, in the late summer of 1918, that a British tanker ship passing offshore was torpedoed by a German U-boat, though some believe it struck a mine laid there earlier. The attack was easily seen by the watchman on the observation tower at the station, for secondary explosions on the ship caused the cargo of gasoline on board to spread over the waves, where it quickly caught fire, the flames leaping high into the air. Six members of the lifesaving crew at the station launched their surfboat despite the fires and headed for the sinking ship. The crew of the sinking vessel managed to board three lifeboats; one of them headed for shore, but another one drifted aimlessly out of control through the inferno while the third one overturned, casting the sailors into the flaming seas. The Coast Guard crew managed to rescue the survivors, despite being exposed to the overwhelming heat that scorched the paint on their rescue boat. It was bravery beyond imagination, and after several hours of rescue efforts, forty-two of the British sailors were brought safely to shore. The rescuers from the Chicamacomico station were decorated by the king

A 650-foot temporary bridge, placed across New Inlet after Hurricane Irene, withstood the power of Hurricane Sandy one year later, although sand covered the highway at both ends. (Courtesy of North Carolina Department of Transportation Photogrammetry)

of England and also received the U.S. Gold Lifesaving Medal of Honor. All six heroes were also awarded the Grand Cross of the American Cross of Honor, of which only eleven have ever been granted. The ship, the SS *Mirlo*, joined the countless other vessels lining the bottom of the sea in the area, giving its name to the nearby beach at Rodanthe so it and the rescue of its crewmen may be forever remembered. The rescue boat, known as No. 1046, can still be seen at the museum there. Stories of the history of the station line the walls of the museum and are worth reading.

Hatteras Island Fishing Pier is less than a mile farther south, and NC 12 leaves Rodanthe shortly after passing the pier. The small town of Waves begins at that point, and there is little noticeable transition between the two villages. Some say the dividing line is a small ditch that runs between the two, but one must look for the town limit signs to be sure. Beaches on both sides of the road are inviting in this area, and campgrounds and rental cottages are plentiful.

The small village of Waves, even smaller than Rodanthe, is soon left behind as the road enters another small community called Salvo. The three towns are so close that they are almost like one town with separate names, and 150 years ago they were, in fact, all part of a community called Chicamacomico. The label, a melodious word believed to be a holdover from a name given by Native Americans, has been misspelled and mispronounced in numerous ways through the years, and none of the derivations were simple, so even in the early years the long stretch of habitation was divided and renamed as North Rodanthe, South Rodanthe, and Clarksville. When post offices appeared on Hatteras Island, one was built for each of the three areas, and, typically for Outer Banks post offices, they gave the villages new names. North Rodanthe became Rodanthe in 1874, Clarksville became Salvo in 1901, and South Rodanthe was changed to Waves in 1939. Local postmasters were allowed to name the post offices where they worked, and they picked names that had meaning for them and the local communities. Eventually, the postal services were combined, leaving just one office in Waves. The Salvo office, reputed to be the smallest post office building in the nation, burned down in 1992, but it has been restored and stands beside NC 12 in red, white, and blue colors today.

Rodanthe has about 400 permanent residents, while Salvo and Waves combined have about half that number. Because development is limited by the boundaries of the Cape Hatteras National Seashore, property is at a premium, and the cottages along NC 12 here have an average value of half a million dollars each. Land so valuable calls for costly cottages,

The nearness of NC 12 to the Atlantic Ocean, as seen in this aerial photograph, exposes the road to washovers along much of its route through hot spots on Hatteras Island, the most fragile part of NC 12. One can see why repairs to the highway are common after even minor storms. (Courtesy of North Carolina Department of Transportation Photogrammetry)

Through rain, sleet, dark of night, and storm-bred waves, the mail still gets through on Hatteras Island. (Courtesy of the Outer Banks History Center, Drew Wilson Collection)

and the road is bordered by expensive scenery as it passes through the three towns. Thirteen miles of open surroundings define the next part of NC 12, where no towns and no development exist. The zone is part of the National Seashore and deserving of the label National Scenic Byway. Tall trees grew here once but were cut for lumber and hauled away on a temporary railroad many years ago, long before the protection of a national park was approved. One of the trestles for that railroad can still be seen near New Inlet, off to the west of the temporary bridge and near the waters of the sound. After the trees were gone, the area, called Kinnakeet Banks, was left exposed, and sand dunes marched across the region from ocean to sound at the will of the wind. A town eventually grew there, and when it got a post office in 1873, the village officially became Kinnakeet. But within ten years, the lyrical Native American name was changed to Avon, and it has been called that ever since.

Avon was a town of considerable industry in the early years. The fishing trade flourished at one time, for the fish were plentiful in both the ocean and the sound waters. Eel-

A few artificial dunes are all that stand between NC 12 and the Atlantic Ocean on Pea Island, and they provide little protection when storms strike the Outer Banks. (Courtesy of the Outer Banks History Center, Aycock Brown Collection)

grass that grew abundantly in the nearby sounds was harvested and baled for sale to be used in stuffing mattresses. As many as forty locals were employed in the gathering of eelgrass. Because oaks and cedars grew there, too, it became a construction site for fishing boats. The type of boat built there had its origins on Roanoke Island, where it was designed and produced by George Washington Creef and the Dough family before others learned to reproduce the design up and down the Outer Banks. The boat was unique and suited for plying the shallow sound waters, thus benefitting the fishermen who caught tons of shad there every year. The boat had a jib and a mainsail, but one thing making it different from other small boats in the region was a small, triangular topsail. It had a

Although storms threaten NC 12 due to the narrowness of Hatteras Island, numerous cottages and other structures lie between the road and the waves in the small villages, resulting in massive damage to property when hurricanes hit. (Courtesy of North Carolina Department of Transportation Photogrammetry)

shallow draft and was highly maneuverable and fast, making it ideal for sailing the waters of the sounds. It was distinctive to the Outer Banks region, and because shad fishermen used it so much, it became known as a "shad boat."

In 1930 a scourge of parasites attacked the eelgrass, almost eliminating it entirely and, consequently, its local harvesting. It also caused a decrease in the number of brant geese that depended on it as a food source, along with the scallops that relied on it too. The advent of motorized boats pretty much eliminated the shad boat, leaving that industry to die out in the early years of the twentieth century, although the state of North Carolina named the shad boat as the official state boat in 1987.

Avon, like many of the other towns on Hatteras Island, came more and more to rely on tourism as its source of income, as well as on the highway that supported that commerce. The town, less than a square mile in area, has 800 residents, is still a fishing center, and has many rental cottages. Dunes no longer sweep through the area despite the lack of tall trees, but NC 12, the road that Avon helped inspire, passes through on its way between Oregon Inlet and Hatteras village.

NC 12 traverses undeveloped areas of the National Seashore to the south of Avon, and within a couple of miles it comes to a famous surfing location on Pamlico Sound known as the Canadian Hole. On a good day, kiteboards and sailboards flutter like colorful butterflies in the wind as surfers dart back and forth over the sound at the site named for the many Canadians who once converged there. A census today might not show a predominance of Canadians, for the Hole is famous around the world, and thousands of visitors surf there every year during the peak season when the sound waters are calm and often bear a favorable wind.

Once past the Canadian Hole, NC 12 continues through about three miles of unspoiled island terrain. On a clear day, the spiraling black and white stripes of the Cape Hatteras Lighthouse can be seen in the distance before the road turns quickly to the west and enters the town of Buxton. The bend is the first sharp curve in the highway after crossing the Bonner Bridge and leads to a region with commercial development of an extent unseen on Hatteras Island so far. The population of Buxton is roughly equal to the combined total of all the Hatteras Island towns we have passed through since crossing Oregon Inlet. Population figures are uncertain on the Banks since some villages are unincorporated, but according to census figures offered by the Outer Banks Chamber of Commerce on Roanoke Island, the total population of the Outer Banks is somewhere between 25,000 and 30,000—a significant number for an area where only dozens or at most hundreds of people once struggled to survive. Even the Native American population probably was never more than a few hundred. It clearly shows the impact of the development of NC 12.

The beach is less obvious here, for the island is wider than usual near Cape Hatteras Point, where the Outer Banks reach their maximum breadth of nearly four miles. The proximity of the cape, which juts out close to the Gulf Stream, supports a warm climate that encourages the growth of maritime forest throughout the town and its surroundings. Growth of such profusion has not been seen since Duck, and even that area would struggle to compete with the local maritime forest surrounding Buxton. The cottages and businesses that exist here in such large numbers are sometimes obscured by the significant foliage, but beside the road, they are readily exposed. The density of the population and the traffic keeps speed limits at twenty-five miles per hour from one end of town to the other.

The nearness of Cape Hatteras caused the village to be known once as simply "the Cape," but after the post office was built there in 1873, it was renamed Buxton for Ralph P. Buxton of Cumberland County, a delegate to the Constitutional Convention of 1875 and later a judge on the North Carolina Superior Court. Perhaps there is no place on the Outer Banks as famous for its fishing as Cape Hatteras, also known as the Blue Marlin Capital of the World. Travel is heavy along NC 12 in Buxton during the best fishing season, which runs for almost a year from springtime until January, when the cold finally drives the fish away.

Nearly five miles south of Buxton, NC 12 enters a narrow village that extends for some length along the road. Popular for its fishing, it was once known as Trent Woods, or simply Trent, until the post office arrived there in 1898, when it became Frisco. According to David Stick in *The Outer Banks*

Sand and debris from wrecked cottages covered NC 12 after the Ash Wednesday Storm struck in 1962. (Courtesy of the Outer Banks History Center, Ash Wednesday Storm Collection)

It is sometimes difficult to locate NC 12 in the aftermath of storms on the Outer Banks. (Courtesy of the Outer Banks History Center, Ash Wednesday Storm Collection)

When Hurricane Isabel struck the Outer Banks in 2003, the storm, like a scythe, carved a swath of destruction across Hatteras Island and NC 12 half a mile wide between Frisco and Hatteras. The gap was so wide that NCDOT considered bridging it rather than restoring the paved road. (Courtesy of North Carolina Department of Transportation Photogrammetry)

of North Carolina, the similarity of the name to Trenton, a post office on the North Carolina mainland, inspired the government to rename it Frisco, supposedly a shortening of San Francisco. (Since the local postmaster had recently visited San Francisco, it was no surprise and a logical choice.) Just a mile or so inside the town limits, NC 12 passes close to the Billy Mitchell Airport and the Native American Museum, which sits right by the highway. Maritime growth gives the town a sheltered image, unlike the open, exposed regions north of Buxton, and the growth protects NC 12 so it is less battered by storms or the ocean. Thus, its pavement has not been continually restored and replaced like the pavement farther north, leaving the asphalt older and showing wear from traffic. It seems a little ironic that NC 12 is rougher in the spots where it has been more protected.

After leaving Frisco, NC 12 leads into another five miles of open territory before coming to the last of the seven small towns along the fifty miles of road that span Hatteras Island. The place is Hatteras, a rare town on the island since it is the only one that has not had its name changed through the ages, even when its post office arrived in 1858. According to Stick, it was likely named for the Hatterask Tribe of Native Americans who once came here to hunt and fish, and it has a population of about 500. At Hatteras, NC 12 comes to a stop for the first time since Corolla. Although the road does not really end here, a ferry connection is necessary to continue along its path.

The ferry landing at the southern tip of NC 12 on Hatteras Island usually has a few cars waiting in line for the next boat ride that will carry them over Hatteras Inlet to Ocracoke Island. But the free ferry ride is short, as is the wait. The Graveyard of the Atlantic Museum sits right around the corner and is worth a visit while one waits. Usually the ride lasts only about half an hour between the two disjointed parts of NC 12, but when storms Irene and Sandy washed large amounts of sand into the channel, long detours were required until the channel could be cleared.

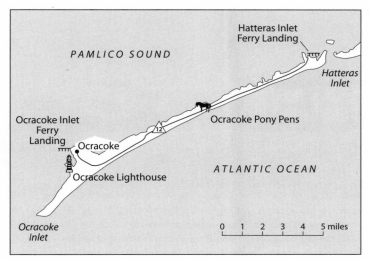

Ocracoke Island

The Drive along Ocracoke Island

After the brief ride aboard the ferry, travelers reach Ocracoke Island, the last part of the Outer Banks spanned by NC 12. The final segment of NC 12 on the Outer Banks skirts the western side of Ocracoke Island through more than a dozen miles of unspoiled wilderness. The only town on the narrow island, the village of Ocracoke, is at the very southwestern tip. From the Hatteras Inlet ferry landing to the lower end of the island, much is still untamed country, probably not much different from when Blackbeard and other pirates sailed past it 200 years ago. Shown on maps from the 1700s as Woccocon, the island later appeared as Wococock and Occacock before appearing as Ocracoke on a map in 1852. Along the way, there were at least a dozen other variations on the name. According to David Stick, the island was named for the Woccon Tribe, a local Native American tribe that once hunted, fished, and lived there. If they were still around today, they likely would not recognize their name, but it has remained Ocracoke for more than one and a half centuries.

When a loose barge collided with the Herbert C. Bonner Bridge, it knocked out a section of the span that was almost as long as a football field, cutting off travel to and from Hatteras Island, other than by ferry, for several weeks. (Courtesy of the Outer Banks History Center, Drew Wilson Collection)

Ocracoke Island stands alone, isolated from both the rest of the Outer Banks and the mainland and pretty much untouched by human development. A little more than a quarter mile wide for most of its length, the sixteen-mile-long island is separated from Hatteras Island by about two miles and from the nearest mainland port by about twenty-five miles. It is the least populated and the least visited of the three major regions of the Banks. Almost all of Ocracoke Island has been protected as part of the Cape Hatteras National Seashore for more than half a century, and it also is part of the National Scenic Byway. Creeks, bogs, woodlands, and white beaches are found along NC 12 between the two ferry landings at the opposite ends of the island. Seven creeks cross the island, where cranes, herons, and egrets glide over the swampy environs or stand one-legged in the dark waters, where they can sometimes be seen from the highway. The Ocracoke Pony Pens are found about half way down the road and hold the only other herd of the Outer Banks mustangs still around. Just as with the ponies at Corolla, it was the paving of NC 12 that threatened the herd and forced them into confinement.

With a goodly portion of the Bonner Bridge missing, automobiles could no longer get across Oregon Inlet, but boats could pass, including those assisting with construction. (Courtesy of the Outer Banks History Center, Drew Wilson Collection)

Heavy equipment was needed to hoist the large pieces required for repairing the Bonner Bridge. Notice the size of the support columns holding the bridge in place. (Courtesy of the Outer Banks History Center, Drew Wilson Collection)

The village of Ocracoke appears magically, almost like a mirage, on the horizon as it looms above the marshy surroundings about eleven miles from the Hatteras Inlet ferry landing. The stretch of NC Highway 12 that leads down the island is named for former Hyde County commissioner Irvin S. Garrish, who resided here in a home believed to have been built by or for his father, Simon Garrish Jr. The house still stands in the town of Ocracoke.

The Irvin S. Garrish Highway makes a long curving turn to the right as it enters the town from the northeast. The old-fashioned village is blessed with a few shaded, quiet streets where live oaks and even fig trees grow around the quaint cottages. It is like a village of yesteryear. Some of the small, narrow streets were paved when the military was based here during World War II, long before NC 12 connected the village with Hatteras Island. The ten-foot-wide pavement of the military roads is barely wide enough to accommodate a single vehicle, so travel along the older streets is slow, befitting the lifestyle of the village.

The whitewashed Ocracoke Lighthouse, visible from town, is the oldest operating lighthouse in the state and the second oldest in the nation. If you want to experience life as it used to be on North Carolina's barrier islands, Ocracoke Island is the place that comes closest. Atypically, it was visitors to the village who sought to maintain the old-fashioned nature of the town by opposing the placement of a highway there back in the 1950s, while the locals were eager for it to be built. Several museums help preserve the image of the past, as does a 200-acre historic district around the harbor where older homes have been preserved. Despite the presence of NC 12, old ways still permeate the town and the island. One is more likely to hear the legendary Outer Banks brogue spoken among residents in Ocracoke than anywhere else along NC 12.

As the highway reaches the southwestern outskirts of the charming town, it approaches the Ocracoke Inlet ferry landing. The Ocracoke Island Visitor Center, operated by the National Park Service, stands close by the ferry docks and offers

The repaving of NC 12 is a constant and ongoing requirement for workers and equipment. Heavy equipment is kept at critical hot spots along its route. (Courtesy of the Outer Banks History Center, Drew Wilson Collection)

guidance to those entering or leaving town. The docks themselves are located on the edge of Silver Lake, known locally as "the Creek" since it was once Cockle Creek until dredged into a lake by the government to create a harbor during the Depression, then scooped out again during World War II to allow the navy to bring in ships. The almost circular lake is situated not far from the center of town. A narrow passage leads out of the lake and into Pamlico Sound to allow ferries to arrive and depart.

Ocracoke is a unique part of the Outer Banks, and even the U.S. Postal Service refrained from renaming it, although it is said to have also been called Pilot Town in its early years before the 1800s for the many boat pilots who lived there. Ocracoke Inlet's importance as a shipping channel for the mainland diminished after the hurricane of 1846 opened Hat-

At Kitty Hawk, despite it being a wide part of the Outer Banks, storms pile sand over NC 12, blocking travel until it can be removed. (Courtesy of the Outer Banks History Center, Drew Wilson Collection)

teras Inlet sixteen miles farther north, but eventually even that was pretty much abandoned when movement by ship to and from the mainland through the Outer Banks became less important.

The End of the Trail

The ferry landing at Ocracoke marks the end of the Outer Banks portion of NC Highway 12, but the road does have one other small section on the mainland connecting the Beach Road with a major U.S. highway. A toll ferry from Ocracoke delivers vehicles and visitors to Cedar Island twenty-five miles away. From there, twelve more miles of NC 12 extend across marshy lowlands and past archaic homesteads like those once seen on the Outer Banks. At US Highway 70, NC 12 ends abruptly. Only then does one get the feeling that the Outer Banks trip is truly over. It was a voyage half a century long for the highway itself and one much shorter for travelers driving on it today, but in either case, it is a remarkable journey that is unlikely to be forgotten.

EPILOGUE

And don't think for a moment that the changes
are at an end. Not by a long shot; they will continue as long as
the waves wash on the beach and as long as the wind blows
the sand around. —Carl Goerch in Ocracoke

It has been almost ninety years since Wash Baum led the campaign to connect the Outer Banks with the rest of the world. The progress of that venture has been unbelievably successful, not only due to the bridge he sponsored but also because of the road-building episodes that followed. Barrier islands that appear to have been flung outward from the North Carolina mainland by some giant hand have been both connected to their home state and perpetually linked to one another by a paved roadway that was once considered impossible to build. For there were no rocks on which to construct a fixed highway firmly and permanently—only an apparently bottomless bed of sand squeezed into meager widths by vast stretches of water on both sides, a sinuous and supple strip of earth that has been formed and reformed by nature and weather through the millennia as it has fought to survive. Yet that road exists, held together in its various parts by bridges and ferries and called NC Highway 12. It is a road that, despite its diminutive dimensions in both width and length, is known throughout the world, for it has brought the vast beauty and opportunities offered by the Outer Banks within the reach of all. Wash Baum served his county well, and the adjoining counties that claim parts of the Outer Banks, too, and he ultimately helped all who wish to visit and enjoy life there.

It took more than fifty years of intermittent spurts of construction for the Beach Road known as NC 12 to be completed

The Cape Hatteras Lighthouse was moved about a half mile inland to keep it from being washed away by encroaching waves that continue to endanger NC 12. (Courtesy of the Outer Banks History Center, David Stick Collection)

on the Outer Banks. No one can say if it will be there for another fifty years, but significant efforts by the North Carolina Department of Transportation, the U.S. National Park Service, and the federal government, along with numerous contractors and workers, have maintained it through a multitude of attacks from nature and intense use during the twentieth century and now in the twenty-first century. Today, the road still travels along the fraying thread of sand called the Outer Banks, representing the only avenue that allows locals and outsiders to traverse the spectacular region.

The Banks themselves linger tentatively, mixing freely with the waters from many square miles of the ocean and sounds that surround them. Water and sand often exchange

NC 12 is a good road as it runs the length of Hatteras Island, connecting Oregon Inlet with Hatteras Inlet, but sometimes waves cross the pavement in low areas when the tide is in, interfering with traffic flow. (Courtesy of the Outer Banks History Center, Drew Wilson Collection)

places, disrupting the silhouette of the island chain as well as the artifacts of human occupation that dare to stand there, but ultimately, the Banks restore themselves to their former status and await the next storm that will surely come their way. NC 12 can only sit and wait for the next assault by wind and wave.

Hope for the future of the Outer Banks and for NC 12 is contingent not only upon tempests but upon the impact of changing sea levels. The seas are rising, and whether this is due to natural fluctuations or a combined result of nature and mankind, the escalation seems more rapid now. The warming of the globe continues as the earth emerges from the last Ice Age, and in the interim, North Carolina and its highway maintenance groups stand literally in the breaches as they attempt to keep the roadway open for travel.

Predictions of future sea-level rises are varied, but none are limited to small changes. And the rate of increase has

Even today, vehicles can become stuck after leaving NC 12, and rising waters can still wreak havoc on any vulnerable mode of transportation. (Courtesy of the Outer Banks History Center, Aycock Brown Collection)

grown over the past three decades. The portent of all this change is that oceans may be as much as two to three feet higher by the beginning of the next century. Low-lying land near the coasts, especially flat beaches where a small difference in the depth of water generates a much larger variation in its inland reach, are vulnerable to flooding, erosion, and even complete disappearance, not to mention the man-made structures that sit there. Estimates are that tens of thousands

Once NC 12 reached Corolla, construction of luxurious cottages began immediately, as can be seen here in the shadow of the Currituck Lighthouse. (Courtesy of the Outer Banks History Center, Drew Wilson Collection)

of miles of roadways lie within the danger zone in the United States, and a couple of those thousands lie along the eastern coast from Maryland to North Carolina, including the highway called NC 12.

Even today, the annual costs of maintenance for NC 12 run into the millions of dollars, especially after severe storms, but that is only a small fraction of the revenue that comes to the state each year through tourism and taxes as a direct result of the existence of that road. Commerce along the Outer Banks is estimated to reach nearly $1 billion a year, so the highway seems to be a good investment.

Local residents, visitors, and North Carolina state officials all recognize the importance of NC 12 on the Outer Banks, but none wants its continuation to imperil the existence of the Banks themselves. For that reason, new techniques are planned by NCDOT to allow the road to be maintained and still allow natural overflow during flooding from storms and waves. These new procedures are meant to be instituted within a couple of years in hopes of preserving NC 12 and the Outer Banks simultaneously.

Wild ponies once roamed free on Ocracoke Island and in the village of Ocracoke itself, but they eventually had to be confined for their own safety. Today, the remaining members of the Ocracoke herd are penned in an enclosure halfway down the road between the two ferry docks. (Courtesy of the Outer Banks History Center, Aycock Brown Collection)

No one can predict with certainty what changes are yet to come along the Outer Banks, but North Carolina will exert whatever efforts are required to keep NC 12 open and safe for travel. Thousands of locals need a road that will permit them to get to their jobs, their schools, and their doctors and to get off the islands if storms threaten. Millions of tourists want to be able to get there and then leave again.

If the daily use of NC 12 by residents and visitors was not enough justification for the continued existence of that road, then one must consider what happens when storms strike the Outer Banks. If future storms of super power like Irene and Sandy hit directly, it will be important to get as many people out of the reach of danger as possible. Work is under way to discover or invent methods that will give ample advance warning to people on the Outer Banks and encourage them to leave when so advised. The Outer Banks highway, NC 12, will play a vital role in any plan of action, for it is the main, if not the only, way to escape weather-related danger.

Some believe that humankind has affected climate change, and there is evidence to support that theory, but cyclical climate change has recurred throughout history even before humans walked the earth. It is doubtful that radical climate alteration is going to be controlled completely by human beings no matter how much one might wish it to be so. The output of climate-influencing gases from a single, large volcano has been measured to be as great in a single day as the expulsion of methane, carbon dioxide, and other impurities from human sources in a year—but none of these additions to the atmosphere do the world any good. It is still possible that humans can control some of their production of hazardous by-products that affect the climate and thereby slow the rate of the melting of glaciers and ice formations around the globe. It is a cause worthy of all our efforts. It is imperative that we do what we can to manage climate change or adapt to it, including trying to preserve the natural and man-made structures we enjoy. That should include the Outer Banks and their highway.

Many things have changed on the Outer Banks since the introduction of a highway there, but not all are directly related to the existence of NC 12. In the early years, residents made their living from fishing, raising cattle, whaling, salvaging wrecks, and a little farming. Lumbering, lifesaving, boatbuilding, and harvesting of marsh grasses were sources of income, too. Today, most of those enterprises have vanished. Few if any shipwrecks end up on the beaches or grounded on the shoals, cattle are no longer allowed on most parts of the Outer Banks, and only a few gardens are still tended for local food supplies. Eelgrass has made a comeback, but no one harvests it for stuffing mattresses anymore. Internal combustion engines have replaced sails as a means of boating about the sounds and ocean, leading to the demise of the shad boat industry. Though fishing is still an active occupation for some, it is mostly to accommodate the tourist trade. The numerous lifesaving or Coast Guard stations that once dotted the Banks at critical locales are almost all gone now, so fewer residents are employed by the federal government to watch over the once-infamous threatening shoals of the Graveyard of the Atlantic.

As old occupations have vanished, new sources of income have arisen—stemming mostly from the presence of NC 12, since it brings the tourists who need goods and services. The tourist industry provides employment and income for many permanent residents today, and the increased need for workers during the busy warm season brings in still others when employment demands exceed the capacity of the local population.

NC Highway 12 helps to meet the changing economic needs of the modern Outer Banks, but it cannot restore the lost lifestyles that have disappeared from their shores. Some still rue the loss of the old ways and would restore them if they could. In places like Hatteras and Ocracoke Islands, where old scenic views and the wild, natural environment stir memories of earlier, simpler times, it is easy to desire a return to the past.

With or without NC 12, the chances are remote that the Outer Banks will ever return to their previous status. The old ways are gone, unlikely to return; bygone days and many former traditions have faded into history, much like the hundreds of sailing craft that lie submerged in the Graveyard of the Atlantic, never to be seen again.

Tall ships no longer sail past the Banks, and few if any modern vessels end up grounded on Diamond Shoals. The coded flashes of lighthouses still warn as they did in olden times, and the Coast Guard stands always ready, but there are few calls today to rescue crews of lost vessels.

David Stick sits at his typewriter on the Outer Banks. He was the recognized authority on the history of the Banks and wrote several popular books that are still in print today. (Courtesy of the Outer Banks History Center, Aycock Brown Collection)

Known by locals as the Beach Road, NC 12 runs the entire length of the Outer Banks. Starting at the southern end of Ocracoke Island within sight of the Ocracoke Lighthouse, it ends in Corolla, a hundred miles or so to the north. (Courtesy of Johnny Horne, photographer)

U-Boats have ceased to prowl just offshore, daring ships to pass. Pirates will not be found in the hidden inlets or coves that once served as their haven. Fishermen are not sailing their shad boats and sharpies across the waters today in the struggle to support their families. Large herds of wild mustangs that once roamed free no longer graze along the marshes, frolic over the sands, or wade into the ocean to escape mosquitoes. Oxcarts are seen only in museums, and then without the oxen. Few tall trees grow on the Banks, even in the preserved areas.

Thousands of residents still call the Outer Banks home, some living in houses as much as a hundred years old that were built from the salvaged timbers and furnishings of wrecked ships. Those who are not fortunate enough to live in that idyllic place must travel there to experience the pleasures offered by both the new and the old of North Carolina's

Like a line drawn in the sand, NC 12 marks a straight and narrow path along Hatteras Island, hardly a presence remarkable enough to either threaten the Outer Banks or to indicate the true significance of the road in the history of the barrier islands. (Courtesy of the Outer Banks History Center, Aycock Brown Collection)

barrier-island chain. Travelers continue to depend on the bridges installed by Outer Bankers so long ago, and on the highway called NC 12 that stretches from one end of the sliver of sand to the other, for the Outer Banks, though in many ways different from what they once were, are as interesting and inviting as ever.

NC Highway 12 has changed the face of the Outer Banks, influenced life there for residents, and made visitation possible in ways hardly dreamed of in years gone by. It has enriched the region and the state, eased the travel needs of locals, and brightened the lives of countless tourists. Equally important, the highway forestalled plans to turn the Outer

Banks into a radioactive, nuclear wasteland—and for that alone, it deserves some respect.

It is possible that the Outer Banks will disappear at some future date. They were not always there; they have come and gone through the millennia like the Ice Ages that are surely tied to their existence. For as long as the Outer Banks remain healthy and intact, they and their highway will coexist in a mutually supportive relationship that most would probably like to see endure, and until the time that the precious ribbon of sand is no more, NC 12 will offer an invitation to all who want to enjoy North Carolina's famous barrier-island chain. It is a transient opportunity whose longevity remains in doubt.

But as North Carolina author, historian, and radio personality Carl Goerch envisioned more than fifty years ago, the wind is still blowing across the sands, and the waves yet wash over the dunes. Wild geese and ducks continue to fly to the Outer Banks every winter, and the beaches are as inviting as ever. Fish swim in the sounds and the sea in such numbers as to attract fishermen from around the world. The fertile marshes stretch over vast areas, where their shallow waters and undulating grasses offer refuge for many forms of wildlife. The rhythmic pounding of Atlantic waves against the lengthy shoreline can be heard all along these barrier islands; some have called it their heartbeat. Until that heartbeat stops, the Outer Banks will live, and with them, their highway, NC 12.

SOURCES FOR FURTHER READING

Adams, Kevin. *Backroads of North Carolina: Your Guide to Great Day Trips and Weekend Getaways.* New York: Voyageur Press, 2009.

Alexander, John, and James Lazell. *Ribbon of Sand: The Amazing Convergence of the Ocean and the Outer Banks.* Chapel Hill: University of North Carolina Press, 2000.

Bachman, Karen. *Insiders Guide to North Carolina's Outer Banks.* 28th edition. Kearney, Neb.: Morris Book Publishing, LLC, 2007.

Baird, Al. *North Carolina's Ocean Fishing Piers: From Kitty Hawk to Sunset Beach.* Charleston, S.C.: The History Press, 2011.

Ballance, Alton. *Ocracokers.* Chapel Hill: University of North Carolina Press, 1989.

Ballentine, Todd. *Tideland Treasure: The Naturalist's Guide to the Beaches and Salt Marshes of Hilton Head Island and the Southeastern Coast.* Rev. ed. Columbia: University of South Carolina Press, 1991.

Barfield, Rodney. *Seasoned by Salt: A Historical Album of the Outer Banks.* Chapel Hill: University of North Carolina Press, 1995.

Barnes, Brooks M., and Barry R. Truitt. *Seashore Chronicles: Three Centuries of the Virginia Barrier Islands.* Charlottesville: University of Virginia Press, 1997.

Barnes, Jay. *North Carolina's Hurricane History.* Chapel Hill: University of North Carolina Press, 1995.

Bishir, Catherine. *The "Unpainted Aristocracy": The Beach Cottages of Old Nags Head.* Raleigh: N.C. Division of Archives and History, 1987.

Butler, Lindley S. *Pirates, Privateers, and Rebel Raiders of the Carolina Coast.* Chapel Hill: University of North Carolina Press, 2000.

Carson, Rachel. *The Edge of the Sea.* Boston, Mass.: Houghton Mifflin Company, 1956.

DeBlieu, Jan. *Hatteras Journal.* Golden, Colo.: Fulcrum, Inc., 1987.

Downing, Sara. *Hidden History of the Outer Banks.* Charleston, S.C.: The History Press, 2013.

Duckett, Randall H., and Maryellen K. Duckett. *100 Secrets of the Carolina Coast: A Guide to the Best Undiscovered Places along the*

North and South Carolina Coastline. Nashville, Tenn.: Rutledge
Hill Press, 1958.

Dunbar, Gary. *Historical Geography of the North Carolina Outer
Banks.* Baton Rouge: Louisiana State University Press, 1958.

Fisher, Allen, Jr. *America's Inland Waterway: Exploring the Atlantic
Seaboard.* Washington, D.C.: National Geographic Society, 1973.

Federal Writers' Project of the Federal Works Agency Work Projects
Administration. *North Carolina: A Guide to the Old North State.*
Chapel Hill: University of North Carolina Press, 1939.

Frankenberg, Dirk. *The Nature of the Outer Banks: A Guide to the
Dynamic Barrier Island Ecosystem from Corolla to Ocracoke.*
Chapel Hill: University of North Carolina Press, 1995.

Garber, Pat. *Ocracoke Wild: A Naturalist's Year on an Outer Banks
Island.* Boone, N.C.: Parkway Publishers, Inc., 2006.

Goerch, Carl. *Ocracoke.* Raleigh, N.C.: Edwards and Broughton
Company, 1956.

Gosner, Kenneth L. *A Field Guide to the Atlantic Seashore from the
Bay of Fundy to Cape Hatteras.* Boston, Mass.: Houghton Mifflin
Company, 1978.

Hines, Sally Nixon. *Coming Home.* Mustang, Okla.: Tate Publishing,
2010.

Lawson, John. *A New Voyage to Carolina.* Chapel Hill: University of
North Carolina Press, 1967.

MacNeill, Ben Dixon. *The Hatterasman.* Winston-Salem, N.C.: John F.
Blair, Publisher, 1958.

Manuel, John. *The Natural Traveler along North Carolina's Coast.*
Winston-Salem, N.C.: John F. Blair, Publisher, 2003.

Meyer, Peter. *Nature Guide to the Carolina Coast.* Wilmington, N.C.:
Avian-Cetacean Press, 1991, 1994, 1998, 2001.

Morris, Glenn. *North Carolina Beaches.* Chapel Hill: University of
North Carolina Press, 1993, 1998.

Morrison, H. Robert, and Christine Eckstrom Lee. *America's Atlantic
Isles.* Washington, D.C.: National Geographic Society, 1981.

Parent, Laurence. *Scenic Driving North Carolina.* 2nd edition.
Guilford, Conn.: Morris Book Publishing, LLC, 2006.

Pilkey, Orrin, Tracy Rice Monegan, and William J. Neal. *How to Read
a North Carolina Beach.* Chapel Hill: University of North Carolina
Press, 2004.

Poyer, David. *Happier Than This Day and Time: An Oral History of the
Outer Banks of North Carolina.* N.p.: Northhampton House, 2012.

Sakowski, Carolyn, and others. *Travel North Carolina: Going Native in the Old North State.* Winston-Salem, N.C.: John F. Blair Publisher, 2004.

Sandberg, Jack. *Uncle Jack's Outer Banks.* Chapel Hill, N.C.: Professional Press, 1998.

Sanders, Keith. *Outer Banks of North Carolina.* N.p.: The Daily Advance, 1974.

Simpson, Bland. *Ghost Ship of Diamond Shoals: The Mystery of the Carroll A. Deering.* Chapel Hill: University of North Carolina Press, 2002.

Simpson, Bland, and Scott Taylor. *The Coasts of Carolina: Seaside to Sound Country.* Chapel Hill: University of North Carolina Press, 2010.

Stick, David. *Dare County: A Brief History.* Raleigh: North Carolina Division of Archives and History, 1970.

———. *The Outer Banks of North Carolina, 1584–1958.* Chapel Hill: University of North Carolina Press, 1958.

———. *An Outer Banks Reader.* Chapel Hill: University of North Carolina Press, 1998.

Wright, Renee. *North Carolina's Outer Banks and Crystal Coast: A Great Destination.* Woodstock, Vt.: The Countryman Press, 2008.

Zepke, Terrance. *Coastal North Carolina: Its Enchanting Islands, Towns, and Communities.* Sarasota, Fla.: Pineapple Press, 2004.

Zinn, Donald J. *The Handbook for Beach Strollers from Maine to Cape Hatteras.* Chester, Conn.: The Pequot Press, 1975.

INDEX

Germans, 38
Goerch, Carl, 147, 158
Goldsboro, N.C., 98
Governor Cherry (ship), 61
Governor Umstead (ship), 61
Grand Cross of the American Cross of Honor, 128
Graveyard of the Atlantic, 11, 154
Graveyard of the Atlantic Museum, 138
Great Depression, 19, 22, 26
Greensboro, N.C., 98
Greensboro International Airport, 101
Greenville, N.C., 99
Gulf Stream, 135

Harrison, Charles, W., 25
Hatteras, N.C., 38, 41, 42, 47, 49, 76, 79, 119, 134
Hatteras Inlet, 41, 43, 58, 77, 143, 144
Hatteras Inlet Ferry, 53, 66, 78, 139, 142
Hatteras Inlet Ferry Dock, 42, 43, 53
Hatteras Island, 34, 37, 39–47, 49, 50, 52, 53, 55, 56, 58, 59, 61, 63, 65, 71, 73, 76, 78, 79, 82, 83, 86, 87, 90, 92, 112, 119, 120, 122, 123, 125, 127, 134, 138, 140, 142, 154
Hatteras Island Coast Guard Station, 49
Hatteras Island Fishing Pier, 129
Hatteras Island Highway, 43
Hatteras Island Road, 39
Hatterask Tribe, 2, 138
Hatterasman, The (book) 33
Hayman, Mathias D., 20
Henderson, N.C., 95

Hendersonville, N.C., 95
Herbert C. Bonner (ship), 61
Herbert C. Bonner Bridge, 63–66, 80–83, 85, 88–91, 119, 120, 122, 124, 125, 134
Heritage Park, 107
Hickory, N.C., 98
Hodges, Luther (governor), 61
Hooper, M. V., 20
Hurricane Bertha, 76
Hurricane Earl, 75, 76
Hurricane Floyd, 76
Hurricane Fran, 76
Hurricane Irene, 75, 78–80, 125, 126, 138, 152
Hurricane Isabel, 75, 76, 78
Hurricane Sandy, 75, 76, 80, 126, 138, 152
Hyde County, 98

Ice Age, 8, 75, 149, 158
Ireland, 13
Irvin S. Garish Highway, 142

Jennette's Pier, 119
Jones, Walter B. (U.S. representative), 23
Jones Hill, 106

Kill Devil Hills, N.C., 3, 13, 59, 73, 115, 116
Kinnakeet, 131
Kinnakeet Banks, 131
Kinston, N.C., 98
Kitty Hawk, N.C., 3, 13, 24–27, 34, 65, 73, 93, 107, 110, 114–16
Kitty Hawk Pier, 111

Lexington, N.C., 95
Lindsey Warren (ship), 61
Lost Colony, 2